T0265483

GETTING IT RIGHT THIS TIME

GETTING IT
RIGHT
THIS TIME

*Break Free from Your Hidden
Blocks to Lasting Love*

Orna and
Matthew Walters

alcove
press

Published in the United States by Alcove Press, an imprint of The Quick Brown Fox & Company LLC.

Alcove Press and its logo are trademarks of The Quick Brown Fox & Company LLC.

Library of Congress Catalog-in-Publication data available upon request.
ISBN (hardcover): 978-1-63910-932-6
ISBN (ebook): 978-1-63910-933-3

Cover design by Phillip Pascuzzo

Printed in the United States.

www.alcovepress.com

Alcove Press
34 West 27th St., 10th Floor
New York, NY 10001
First Edition: January 2025
10 9 8 7 6 5 4 3 2 1

This book is for you who is reading this right now. No matter your frustrations, fears, or past experiences with love and dating, we wrote this book to show you the way to create the soul-satisfying, long-lasting love you desire and deserve. You are worth loving.

CONTENTS

INTRODUCTION

How Did You Get Here?

"The greatest thing you'll ever learn is just to love and be loved in return."

—Eden Ahbez

On New Year's Eve 1994, Orna was fighting for her life.

The boyfriend she lived with, who came home drunk, high, or both, was on top of her beating her head into the hardwood floor.

Unable to get out from under the weight of his body, she did what every woman has been taught to do to save her life—she grabbed his balls. When she finally let go, he struck her face so hard that the bodybuilder and his girlfriend next door said they heard it in their apartment. It was the bodybuilder who came through the front door to save Orna's life that night.

Holding her torn pj's closed with one hand, she dialed 911 with the other.

Every single thing in Orna's life changed that night. Most of all, she desired to figure out how she had chosen a man who could be violent when that was the very last thing she wanted in a partner.

A decade later, in her mid-thirties and flourishing in her career, Orna began a quest to figure out how to have a great love relationship, one that would last for a lifetime. It started with meditation. One morning, Orna asked at the close of her practice, "What do I *really* want?" The answer lit up her third eye with a royal purple hue backdrop and L-O-V-E appeared. "NOOOO!" she thought. "I don't know how to do that. Anything but love, it has to be something else. I'm genuinely not good at that. There has to be something else!" she begged God. Day after day it persisted. She'd ask and the same answer came again, and again, and again. By this point in her life, Orna knew the difference between the answers that came from the universe and those in her head. This was like a message from God on the direct-dial red phone line: She wanted LOVE. Gulp!

Reluctant to take it on, Orna realized she could start by doing research, and because she was an expert at research, it would be easier that way—like asking for a friend. Conventional wisdom says to marry someone from a good family. That struck terror in her heart. "No one will ever pick me, then," she thought. "My family is awful." As she consumed all the books about love and dating she could find, took workshops, and went to therapy, the most common takeaway she learned is that lasting love is hard for everyone. But the books she read and workshops she took never addressed the underlying false belief that had driven Orna in her love life for decades: "I am unlovable."

Basically, there was no advice for someone like her who had experienced abuse, chaos, and trauma in her childhood home and was finding it again in her adult love relationships. The physical wounds from that frightful New Year's Eve long healed, Orna desired to know *how* to choose a man who would love her respectfully and work through the challenges that life would inevitably bring, along with attraction, chemistry, and if at all possible, someone who would know how to lighten her up when she took herself too seriously.

While Orna was on her healing journey, Matthew had been through a spiritual awakening. He grew up in a "normal" midwestern family, the youngest of five children: no abuse, no trauma, nothing from the outside that would make you think that finding a great love relationship would be difficult. Yet Matthew also struggled to create lasting love through most of his adult life. He had internalized the teasing from his childhood to mean that there was something wrong with him. Because he didn't like himself, he was always suspicious of a woman who was interested in him. Couldn't she see that there was something wrong with him? He would develop crushes on women who weren't interested in him or who were unavailable for a relationship. All that taunting from his childhood had turned into self-hatred and as a result, Matthew believed he was incapable of sustaining a romantic relationship.

When Matthew met a woman who was interested in him, who thought he was cute and interesting, his first thought was, "What's wrong with her?" and the second was, "Wait 'til you get to know me"—and that usually became a self-fulfilling prophecy. He would inevitably sabotage the relationship. These strategies were exacerbated by recreational drug use and numbing himself out with alcohol. After his self-sabotaging behaviors caused him to lose a good job, Matthew decided it was time to clean up his act.

Sobriety, yoga, meditation, and hypnotherapy helped break his self-destructive and self-sabotaging behaviors, but love continued to elude him. The fear that drove Matthew was: "I don't trust love." It wasn't until a spiritual awakening through meditation that he was able to drop the cynicism that had defined his adult life. The realization that he was the only one responsible for his happiness, and that it was up to him to change his life, prompted Matthew to commit to a practice of self-acceptance and personal responsibility. Slowly but surely, these new practices increased his self-esteem, and he began to turn his love life around. By the time Matthew met Orna, he'd been on an intentional search for the lasting love that he'd rejected outright for most of his adult life. He was ready for love and had begun a search to find his soulmate.

This is just a glimpse of what we went through on our journey to each other. After many experiences that shaped who we became before meeting, and other relationships that didn't pan out, we met through a local business networking group. Matthew was running his hypnotherapy practice in Beverly Hills and an online hypnosis business with a colleague, and Orna had hung her shingle as a life coach utilizing the science of hand analysis (scientific nonpredictive palmistry). We met for a one-on-one networking breakfast after attending the same group meetings for over a year. Enthralled with each other, we sat talking for hours. The shift changed at the restaurant, and a new waiter came to take our lunch order. Flirtations continued for several weeks through the group's networking meetings. During one, a dating coach offered a ticket to her "Date with Fate" program. Matthew turned to Orna and said, "You can have a Date with Fate or you can have a date with me." Matthew won out over fate that day, and we haven't been apart since.

When asked in interviews how Orna knew Matthew was her soulmate, she says, "The obsessive and anxious feelings I used to have at the beginning of a relationship weren't present. I felt grounded in a new way, like I was standing on Mother Earth with deep roots like an oak tree. At the same time, I felt like I had wings and could take flight at any moment. Roots and wings were an entirely new experience of falling in love, one that I didn't know was possible."

While planning our wedding in 2009, we had an opportunity to give a motivational talk together at a new spa in Hollywood. We decided to share our journey to each other and the steps we took to consciously create our relationship. This led to a weekend workshop that grew into our holistic coaching practice Creating Love on Purpose®. Through many years we have refined our system for identifying and transforming hidden blocks to love in addition to teaching the tools to make love last.

Our clients have had success creating long-lasting love regardless of race, culture, gender affiliation, sexual preference, or religion. As a couple with both a fulfilling marriage and a successful practice as holistic dating coaches, we have a life that many people dream of—but our lives weren't always this rosy. The struggles we faced on our journey to one another were frustrating and painful, and hopefully relatable. We're willingly sharing with you our personal pilgrimage to long-lasting love so that you can avoid driving in circles, taking wrong turns, and winding up at dead ends. Within these pages is a tried-and-true method that charts a path to your soulmate relationship. A beloved relationship is not destined. You need *not* scour the earth to find the one person who is your match.

Orna has been told many times to stop telling people she's a survivor of domestic violence. At the time (and for many years after) she thought it would be a secret she'd keep forever.

Now she looks for opportunities to share her story because no one should take on the shame of another person's actions. There's no shame in loving someone. The actions of her ex-boyfriend are something he will have to reconcile for himself. As far as Orna is concerned, she tells the story of New Year's Eve 1994 as often as possible and to anyone who will listen, because domestic violence doesn't discriminate—it can happen to anyone.

And here's what we've discovered: **Love doesn't discriminate, either.** If you have the desire to share your life with an ideal partner, you can create a soulmate relationship. The existence of your desire means it's possible for you. The journey may not be an easy one, but few things in life worth having are effortless. You'll learn how to build your resiliency in love (and as a bonus—it's likely to spill over into other areas of your life). Keep your eye on the prize, not because you *need* to have someone to complete you, but because sharing your life with the love of your life makes everything better! Life may not be fair or just, but having a partner to go through the highs and lows alongside you is a priceless experience, one that is available to everyone—including you.

Whatever your particular struggles with love and dating to this point, your brain has collected evidence to back up your experiences. If you're looking for evidence of love being difficult, it's easy to find: heartbreaking relationships that don't last, the struggle to get your needs met, fear of rejection, unhappy married couples who stay together for one reason or another—all this evidence is working against you. Swapping out one partner for another doesn't improve your chance for success, either. According to Jennifer Baker of the Forest Institute of Professional Psychology, forty-three percent of all first marriages in the United

States, sixty percent of second marriages, and seventy-five percent of third marriages end in divorce. Marriage statistics like this one prove that starting over in a new relationship won't increase your chance for success because people don't get better at lasting love by happenstance.

When people marry, they generally don't expect to end up divorced. So why does it seem nearly impossible for so many people to find and keep a healthy, lasting, loving romantic relationship? The problem lies in the myths our culture has about love—and which you've bought into consciously or unconsciously. All the songs, movies, books, and poems tell you that love is a magical thing that "just happens." You've been taught that your problems with dating and mating lie outside of your control. If you could just find this mystical unicorn person who "gets" you and understands your needs (without you having to articulate them) then you will be one of the "lucky" ones who gets to live happily ever after, right?

Another common myth about love is that the right relationship should be easy and not require any work. A corollary to this myth is that supposedly attraction and common interests are all you need to stay together for a lifetime. Other myths include: *Because love is a mystery, it's just as easy to fall out of love as it is to fall in love. Love will happen when you least expect it. Stop trying so hard; it will happen if it's meant to be. Love is beyond your control.*

But the myth of accidental love is wreaking havoc on your love life. It keeps you from accessing your free will when it comes to love. Expecting your love life to change one day when you meet the right person is the biggest myth perpetuated on you since birth. In order to free yourself from these false beliefs and further heartbreak, you must look at love, dating, and relationships in an entirely new way.

It's time for you to rewire your brain for lasting love with an ideal partner. We'll call this person your soulmate. A soulmate is the person you choose for life who also chooses you. Together, you help heal the wounds of the past and grow together to the highest and best versions of yourselves. A soulmate does not complete you; a soulmate complements you. Ultimately, you are better together than apart. The journey you're going on is designed to allow your personal growth to bring in your beloved life partner.

A soulmate does not complete you; a soulmate complements you.

There are many differing thoughts on soulmates and soulmate relationships; many of them perpetuate the idea that it's your mission in life to find the one person who is fated to be your other half. Others claim that soulmates are destined to break your heart. Some people scoff at the idea of soulmates altogether. Being with your soulmate isn't fated or destined, nor do you have to scour the earth for your one true love. There is no higher power doling out love to some people and not others. Merriam Webster's definition is "a close friend or romantic partner with whom one has a unique deep connection based on mutual understanding and acceptance."

Maybe you thought you met your soulmate and that person broke your heart. The idea that a soulmate is here to jolt you and crack you open as a catalyst for change is an example of what we call a soul contract. We believe you have agreements with other souls (not always a lover), and some of these contracts are played out in the light, and some are played out in the dark. This is not a soulmate relationship at all, but rather someone who is here to move you forward toward your soul's purpose. Soul contracts occur with people who play a role in your journey but who are not your forever person. You could think of them as catalysts for change, prompting you to grow to the next stage of your journey. Are you carrying a torch for someone who got away? Do you think you've missed out on your soulmate?

What you believe to be true is true for you—so how do you change your belief system to create long-lasting, soul-satisfying love? *Getting It Right This Time* is the culmination of all the years of experience guiding singles to create love on their own terms, changing how they select a mate, and growing together rather than apart. Falling in love triggers a dopamine rush of intoxication. But when you approach love consciously, you don't find yourself in old habitual patterns of worry like, "I hope I don't screw this up," or "I'm afraid that I'll be duped again." Plenty went wrong between us in the beginning of our relationship as well as throughout our many years together, but our commitment to each other and to our work helped us to master communication skills and turn conflicts into a deeper connection.

Getting It Right This Time walks you through retraining your brain to unlearn what's no longer serving you and provides you with new strategies for giving and receiving love that are in alignment with your true heart's desire.

Your past does not define you or limit you. If you desire to have a lasting, loving partnership, then that drive is enough to create it. We know this to be true because if we can do it, then anyone can do it, and that includes *you*. Rather than waiting for lasting love to just magically happen one day, make having love a priority, because when you focus on love you'll change your life.

Your journey through *Getting It Right This Time* will traverse three phases: Awareness, Transformation, and Manifestation. *Awareness* is the first step to shining a light on your mental, emotional, and behavioral patterns. Your specific patterns are hidden blocks to the love you desire and deserve. Awareness gets you into the driver's seat of the car. You haven't gone anywhere yet, but you're in the right seat to reach your goal. Examine your patterns with empathy and compassion. Set judgment aside, as it's the biggest block to the love you desire. The past is done; you don't have a time machine, so it does you no good to judge yourself or wallow in regret. You'll soon learn there's a good reason you've struggled in your love life, and until now, it's been hidden from you. Coming into awareness sets the stage for a transformation so you can heal your heart and open to a new way of creating long-lasting love.

Phase two is *Transformation*, which guides you to release limiting beliefs, habits, and behaviors that don't serve the goal of finding your beloved. Your limiting beliefs, false beliefs you've adopted that don't serve your best interests, have hidden the right person from you and have created your current struggle. In the transformation phase, you'll experience an internal shift that will forever change your outer experiences. Instead of undigested knowledge that comes from collecting more information, this journey will integrate new learning into your daily life, and all of your relationships will benefit. Just like riding a bike, once you have a new experience you can't deny it; you'll have integrated the learning on a subconscious level. This transformation puts the past behind you, opening a glorious future filled with new beliefs and skills to attain your goal of sharing your life with your soulmate.

The final phase, *Manifestation*, walks you through creating your vision for a lasting loving partnership and shortens the time it takes to make it a reality. Manifestation isn't just repeating affirmations, or wishful thinking, or hoping that your life will change. Instead, you'll be in the dating lab using your power of discernment to choose the best partner for you. You'll create new coordinates for your personal GPS for love, making it inevitable that you meet your ideal mate. On this journey your goal is to create long-lasting love, not just to have another boyfriend, girlfriend, or lover. This book is *not* a quick fix for meeting your soulmate in 30 days or less. You'll transform false beliefs, break negative patterns, and gain a new skill that allows you to select an ideal life partner and the tools for love to last a lifetime.

Changing behavior doesn't come from having information. You don't walk into a room and decide who you find attractive; it happens on autopilot. There may be a lot of undigested knowledge floating around in your brain that didn't change your results. Our goal is to turn all of that data into experiential learning. Please remember that learning to do anything new takes time and practice. Change doesn't just happen from desire; it takes effort. Embrace all the Love on Purpose Exercises at the close of each chapter. You'll be tasked with writing exercises as well as experiential practices, so you'll need a journal book and your favorite pen or pencil. Please don't use a digital device, as part of the process of creating change is putting pen to paper. Utilize the QR codes at the end of each chapter to gain access to additional resources for success on your journey. Commit to taking new actions consistently, and most importantly—love yourself through this process. All the sages say, "Know thyself." That's because you only have control over what you feel, think, and do; you have no control over other people or the world around you. This simple but profound truth will be the foundation of our work together.

When you harness the power of the brain science of attraction, you'll know how to make your own luck in love. If you're having trouble executing the exercises at the end of a chapter or struggle to commit to the practices on a regular basis, you may want to consider reading the book cover to cover without doing any exercises at all to gain an overview of the journey. Then go back through the book again, reading each chapter and implementing the exercises as you go. It's best that you don't skip around because reading the book out of order dilutes the effectiveness of our Soulmating System™. The order is very important because your inner transformation will shift your outer-world experience (not the other way around). Use any discomfort you're in at the moment when you think of your love life as fuel to make your way through the sequence we've laid out for you. There's not much you can do with a half-baked turkey, so be sure to stay in the oven until it's fully cooked.

Please note: Names and identifying details of all persons have been changed to protect privacy unless the identity is one of us. You'll learn details of our journey to each other, along with many of our clients and their transformations. Your desire for long-lasting love means it's possible for you to create it. Our clients in their mid-twenties to their mid-seventies have achieved their goal of creating lasting love, regardless of their gender identity, sexual preference, culture, religion, or geographical location. Using our techniques, 100 percent of our clients who found their partner and chose to get married are still married today.

When you learn to love yourself, you can teach someone to love you. Approach this journey with optimism, hope, and an open heart, and soon you'll find that you too are creating love on purpose. If your heart is hurting right now, please ride on our faith in you. When you're with your beloved, every step will have been worth it.

When you learn to love yourself, you can teach someone to love you.

PART I

Awareness

I

The Myth of Accidental Love

"And the day came when the risk to remain tight in a bud was more painful than the risk it took to blossom."

—Anais Nin

From childhood, you're taught a ridiculous myth about love that permeates society so thoroughly that you have no choice but to believe that you "fall" in love. You're also told that love will happen when you least expect it. That "when you know, you know." Your belief in the myth of "love by accident" is so powerful that on some level you never completely grew out of the coming-of-age fantasy that one day, while going about your everyday mundane activities, you'll meet an ideal match to be your partner for life. This person will just magically appear if it's meant to be, and the timing will be just right. The two of you will quickly fall madly in love, get married, start a family, and live in bliss happily ever after.

When love by accident doesn't happen for you, you cobble together experiences of disappointment and heartbreak, believing that love must not be in the cards for you because it didn't just magically happen. You may find that your desire for a life partner waxes and wanes like the moon's cycle, and you may even feel apathetic about love and dating altogether. Perhaps

3

you start believing that you're unlucky in love. After all, according to society, when it doesn't work out, it's also not "meant to be."

Everything in life worth having requires effort. You're told to get an education, study, gain skills, practice, and work hard at everything you want—except love. The most important decision in life you leave to chance, like buying a lottery ticket. And the chance of winning the lottery? One in 292 *million.* When you do connect with someone you perceive as having potential, you pine for them to like you back, and maybe try to persuade them to return your affection. This desire to be liked causes you to give your power away to a complete stranger, before you know if the two of you are ideally suited for a long-term relationship or not. When this happens, you place your lovability in the hands of a stranger, giving a person you just met the power to determine your worthiness in love. We call this "dating backward," as you're giving a stranger the benefit of the doubt—all because of a feeling.

Love by accident is guided by your feelings. The way a stranger makes you feel is the most important part of your interaction, and some people go so far as to abandon logic and reason and dive right in investing their heart. So, let's ask you this very important question: Have you ever had a feeling last for any significant period of time? No feeling lasts; they're all temporary. The myth of accidental love has indoctrinated you to select a life partner based on something as fickle as a feeling. You're okay with this because you've been told your whole life to trust those feelings, and if it's the "right" person, it'll work out.

The hard truth is that accidental love is a fantasy.

Having the information (and the experience) that love by accident is a delusion doesn't stop you from behaving as if the fairy tale is true. As proof, when we speak of conscious love, of "Creating Love on Purpose," we are often met with comments like, "But isn't it more romantic when it just happens?" Or people speak of wanting it to happen "organically" as if their dating life is an apple on a tree. The meet-cute at Starbucks may seem more romantic at the beginning, but after the feel-good chemicals wear off, you're left with an imperfect person to share your life with—one you don't feel the same way about as when you first met. It's not enchanting when it doesn't have much chance of lasting and instead is likely to break your heart.

Sure, you've met people who have a romantic story of how they met. Their courtship was full of fun, flirtation, and romantic "accidents." This initial romance stage is important because it puts gas in the tank of the relationship, allowing the couple to move past the second stage of relationship: the power struggle stage. We can assure you that when you connect with your beloved it will *feel* magical—but magic is not a plan.

Long before we met, Orna asked people who had been married for a long time, "What's your secret?" The answers she's received through decades have elements of romance and also reveal conscious choices to put the relationship first, as well as tend to its health and wellbeing. Relationships may start "accidentally" and be full of romance, but without conscious growth, good communication skills, and a commitment to get through challenges together, they'll have a hard time surviving—let alone thriving.

You've experienced elements of love by accident through most of your adult life. Questioning the validity of the myth only occurs once you've experienced issues with the end result—usually a painful breakup or divorce. Waking up from the spell of expecting love to magically last can be like having a glass of cold water thrown in your face. Ideally, this waking-up process is accompanied by the realization that you are the common denominator in all your relationships. The one constant in all your relationships is you—your thoughts, your feelings, and your behavior. By recognizing that you're responsible for the patterns that have steered you wrong, you're now in the driver's seat to create positive change and to get love right.

Matthew woke up from the spell of accidental love in his mid-thirties after a short but very intense experience with a woman he met through a mutual friend. After just two weeks of dating, she told him, "It's best to end this now because I'll just hurt you even more two months from now." The pain he felt in that moment made him acutely aware of his pattern of being attracted to rejection. His desire for this woman increased the more she insisted she wasn't a match for him. Looking back over his past relationships, Matthew noticed that the more unavailable a woman was, the more his attraction for her intensified. It didn't feel right if it was clear a woman was drawn to him. The awareness that rejection felt familiar, somewhat comfortable to him, became the catalyst for Matthew to examine his patterns in his relationships and to begin a quest to break those patterns for good.

The problem with accidental love is that it's incredibly intoxicating. The connection is very intense, as if the other person can see you in a way that no one else can. You believe that you'll never experience this feeling with anyone else. The false positive that comes with love by accident deludes you into thinking you've instantly connected with and recognized your soulmate. The feelings are so strong that you believe this person, this situation, and this romance is unique, different from any other ever experienced by anyone throughout time. Of course, you only need to read a few romance novels to know there is nothing at all unique about it. While romance and sexual chemistry may be intense and intoxicating, they're rarely long-lasting. Like a candle that burns brightly, it only lasts half as long. *Beware of instant intimacy.* An intense connection with a stranger may mean something very different than what you've been led to believe.

This doesn't mean that love on purpose does not include romance and sexual chemistry, as these are essential ingredients in a healthy relationship. It will feel absolutely incredible when you meet your beloved, and you'll have plenty of synchronistic experiences and cherished memories to look back on. The difference is it won't feel like it has in the past because it will be an entirely new experience. Your current expectations of "falling in love" are based on faulty coordinates and have been steering you in the wrong direction your entire life.

Rather than selecting a life partner based on attraction and chemistry alone, there are other components that are necessary to sustain a long-term intimate relationship. Think of relationships like baking bread. Yeast is only one ingredient in the whole recipe, and without it you'd just have a cracker. A cracker would be disappointing if you were hoping for some yummy, soft, chewy bread; therefore, you must have all the ingredients to bake it. Similarly, you cannot forsake sexual chemistry or attraction in a romantic relationship as it's a necessary ingredient for love to last. It may sound like good advice to marry your best friend, that as long as you have the same interests and hobbies in common you'll have what it takes to make love last. Sadly, many of these marriages generally end in divorce because it's impossible to settle for a lifetime.

What if there was another way? What if you could have the spark of attraction and also have a relationship stand the test of time? What if you could spend the rest of your life with your soulmate by your side?

Conscious choice is the most important skill for love to last. As unromantic as that may seem, there's nothing more romantic than waking up every morning and choosing to love the person lying in bed next to you day after day, year after year, decade after decade. *Love is a choice*, and coming to terms with this fact is the first step to activate your free will to take control of your love life. It's the desire for long-lasting love that is fuel to create change.

Conscious choice is the most important skill for love to last.

Often, this desire comes from a recent painful experience. No matter the source of your pain—whether it's seeing all your friends married off and feeling left behind, or your sudden realization that you're stuck in a negative pattern selecting the same kind of person again and again, or if you've recently reached the completion of a difficult divorce from a long marriage, or if you were just dumped out of the blue by someone promising—pain can be a powerful motivator for change. Maybe you started examining your relationship strategies because of heartbreak or loneliness. Having your heart broken is part of the maturation process; it's part of growing up. If you've come to this journey due to heartache, know this can be a powerful catalyst for growth and transformation, and while you may not see it now, it's something you'll be grateful for at the end of your journey.

Desire can also come from something positive, like yearning for more, or something completely new and different. Perhaps you've settled in past relationships and you're in a position to want more from your love life but haven't been able to figure it out on your own. Or maybe you married early before knowing yourself well enough to make a worthy choice (the so-called starter marriage). Society may not support you wanting more than just security and someone who's kind, but we believe that everyone deserves to have a soul-satisfying love relationship that lasts. It's difficult to settle for a lifetime with someone just because they're a good person. Not every kind person will be the right match for you long-term.

Whether it's frustration with dating apps or a history of bad relationships, cynicism about love is a trap that's hard to escape. It can feel like there's no one out there for you or that the universe is conspiring to keep love from you. Inside every cynic is a disappointed romantic, someone who believed in love but was hurt and put on a false coat of cynicism to avoid feeling hurt again. Everyone has had disappointments in life. Not every relationship works out the way you'd like, but that doesn't mean that you must become cynical about life and love. Allow your desire to share your life with someone special to be the fuel that creates resiliency in love.

Society prepares you for setbacks in other parts of your life. You might not get into the college you desire, so you also apply to a few other schools. When looking for a job, you don't put all your hopes and dreams into one position at one company. If you ask for a raise and don't get it, you don't quit and decide you'll find another job where you never have to ask for a raise again. It's the myth of love by accident, yet again, setting you up for disappointment in your love life. Every person you fall for may not fall for you, and that's just the way life is. However, when you discover your patterns in love, you can see what is working for you and what's keeping you stuck in a negative pattern of heartbreak.

When Orna realized that love and pain were intertwined in her subconscious mind, it made sense that she pined for a person she could not have. The familiar pain of feeling unlovable, being the one who was not chosen, was in alignment with what she learned about love in her family of origin. Matthew was teased and ridiculed by his brothers and their friends. As the youngest in a family with five children, he wasn't physically able to keep up with them. The feeling of rejection felt like the love he'd received growing up. It makes sense he was chasing rejection into his thirties.

Awareness of your patterns in love is the first step to changing your results. Do you choose emotionally unavailable partners? Do you try to earn love by sacrificing your own needs and desires? Do you bail when conflict arises? Do you consider yourself responsible for your partner's emotional responses? Do you twist yourself into a pretzel trying to win someone's love and prove your worthiness?

Another common myth about love is that you're *attracting* a particular kind of person, as if there's a magnet inside of you drawing in a specific type of individual (one that is not an ideal match for you long-term). *This is not only incorrect, but also in reverse.* In reality, it's *you* that's the common denominator in all your relationships, so it's you who finds a particular kind of person attractive. It's your mind that's highlighting a familiar dynamic that sparks the feeling of a connection inside of you.

Making a chart of your relationship history brings awareness to the common qualities you're unconsciously attracted to and brings your patterns to light. This isn't a list of your desires in a relationship, nor a list of the qualities of your ideal person; rather, it's an examination of the qualities of the kind of person you've ended up with when leaving love to chance and happenstance. At the end of this chapter we've made it easy for you to chart your relationship history. It's important to identify repetitions, similarities, and parallels, all the clues that bring your specific relationship pattern into focus.

Your attraction patterns as an adult originate from your experience of love in your family of origin. The same people who taught you to walk, talk, and tie your shoes also taught you about love. Long before you knew about yourself or how the world works, you made decisions about what's possible for you in love. The rudder on your very own Love Boat was set with particular coordinates of attraction. These coordinates were set by your childhood experiences with the people who raised you and the meanings you assigned to events when you were a kid.

Discovering your patterns moves you into the seat of your power. You'll no longer be able to blame your struggles in love on your age, where you live, or any of the false beliefs you've convinced yourself are the problem. You have the power to make the necessary changes to heal your heart and move on from the strategies of love by accident to Creating Love on Purpose.

There are similar patterns that we've frequently spotted with our clients. They had a hidden belief system, a flawed piece of software that was driving their behavior and wreaking havoc in their hearts. Once you identify your hidden blocks to love buried inside your attraction patterns, you can never go back to your past strategies of dating and selecting a mate.

One of our clients, Debbie, described herself as a "second mom" to her younger siblings because she helped raise them. Growing up in a very traditional family, sharing feelings was not valued or practiced in her childhood home. Her mother taught her to never "rock the boat" or come across as arrogant by sharing her opinion. Deep down, she held a belief that her needs and desires didn't matter. As an adult, she always acquiesced to the other person's desires to make her relationships work. For decades, Debbie gave in to the demands of her husband and children. After her husband succumbed to cancer, she didn't date for a long time because her adult daughter couldn't bear the thought of her mother dating different men.

When Debbie did start dating (in secret to not upset her daughter), she ended up in a lot of dead-end situations with men who treated her as a convenient friend, none of them moving the relationship forward. Upon the shocking discovery that she was the other woman in a relationship with a man she thought was exclusive with her, she reached out to us. We quickly discovered that Debbie had kept her needs and desires a secret for so long she had no idea what would bring her joy. Before she could feel confident speaking up, she had to get in touch with her feelings and discover her own desires. Learning to speak up and make requests, as well as set healthy boundaries with her adult daughter, gave her the confidence she needed.

With our help, Debbie was able to be more discerning through the dating process. She stopped people pleasing and had a new way to evaluate the guys she was dating. Soon, she met a man who stood out from the rest, and it was clear he was pursuing her for a relationship. He often asked about her preferences and desires, and also did his best to deliver on her requests. The relationship had started out long distance, and within the first year he moved to her city—something that Debbie had never imagined a man would do for her. Even her daughter warmed up to the fact that her mother had a boyfriend and wanted to meet him. Debbie has been exclusively dating him for years now, and they're very happy together.

Keisha reached out to us after her lover became abusive and manipulative. Having grown up in a home filled with abuse, she'd thought that was all behind her after years of therapy. Like many who've suffered abuse, Keisha had been under the impression she could spot an abuser quickly and steer clear of them. She described the attraction for him as electric and intense. We quickly identified that she'd confused these fervid feelings with a soul connection, and because she believed they were "meant to be together" she cut him a lot of slack, resorting to old strategies of sacrificing her needs to please him and unable to draw clear boundaries with him. Even after he cruelly ended the relationship, she would fantasize he'd come back to her. Keisha craved the intense feelings she had with him, like a drug addict who needed their next fix. She insisted they were supposed to be together despite the fact that he was abusive and manipulative and created chaos in her life.

In reality, Keisha's attachment to him meant that she had misinterpreted a fear response as attraction. The physiological response to fear and excitement are exactly the same in the body—heart rate increases, breath becomes shallow, stomach full of butterflies, and palms may get sweaty. It's common for people to confuse fear with excitement, especially when standing in front of a group to give a speech or waiting in line to ride a rollercoaster; however, a victim of abuse misinterprets excitement and attraction with fear.

Clients with a history of toxic relationships have shown us that instant intimacy isn't necessarily an indication of a soulmate connection. Keisha's experience may sound extreme, but it clearly illustrates that there's something else at play through the process of selecting a mate. No matter your relationship history, beware of instant intimacy! The most difficult pattern to break is the attachment to toxic experiences. The fear response is swallowed up and misconstrued as excitement, creating an elixir of feelings that are irresistible.

Many people without a history of toxic relationships struggle to identify a match for long-lasting love. Their situations are not dramatic like Keisha's (or Orna's); instead, their experiences are rather mundane. They either chase rejection or they're stuck in a pattern of selecting emotionally unavailable partners, or they wonder if they can fall in love, or a variety of different patterns that play out without heightened drama and chaos. They still end up alone and frustrated simply by buying into the myth of love by accident. No matter your current situation or past experiences, there's a pattern that belongs to you, and becoming aware of it is essential to create an internal change so you can select the right partner for the long term, not just someone that matches what's familiar to you.

Meeting your beloved should feel calm and easy, like meeting an old friend combined with curiosity. You feel passion and attraction, but it's not overwhelming or all-consuming. You feel grounded, you can think straight, and you can make rational decisions. Your head and your heart are in harmony rather than in conflict. *Love on purpose* means you're not dating like a teenager, you're not a slave to your feelings, and you can be rational and slow down the dating process to evaluate if the person you just met is a match to your desires for a long-term intimate relationship.

Our client Katrin's grandmother lived with her family when she was young. Her grandmother taught her not to burden anyone with her feelings. She learned to model her grandmother by putting on a false face to please others. This left Katrin unable to trust her feelings, and she discounted them by believing her feelings weren't worth sharing. Constantly afraid she'd offend someone, Katrin often found herself in awkward situations with acquaintances. People she just met would share personal information and intimate details with her, and she felt trapped. Unable to speak her mind to get out of these situations, she was frozen while smiling, unconsciously giving a green light for them to continue. Katrin spent years struggling to find an emotional connection while dating and was afraid guys would ask too much of her.

Through our Soulmating System, Katrin learned to identify her feelings, speak her mind, and show up authentically. For the first time in her life, she was comfortable sharing her true self, and everything changed. She felt excited to meet guys and date, she began regularly flirting with strangers on the subway, and her career blossomed. This inner shift inside of her allowed her to be less guarded, and that opened up new opportunities in every part of her life.

Dating while identifying and speaking her feelings changed the selection process for Katrin. She connected with a man who valued her, and after dating for a couple years they married and started a family. This client's transformation is not unique; many people are raised to believe that their feelings are a burden to others. Being authentic means only one thing—to speak your feelings. This is the only way to create an emotional connection with another person and to evaluate an ideal match through the dating process.

What are your patterns and strategies for love? How do you choose a partner? Are you holding on to past hurts and mistakes? Are you afraid to open your heart and be vulnerable while getting to know someone new? Identifying your negative patterns and strategies will move you from bumbling to blossoming in your love life.

You do not have to settle when it comes to love. The goal is not to rush to exclusivity, to get a ring, or to have a wedding—the goal is to share your life with the love of your life. You can accomplish this goal by committing to the journey of love on purpose. The first step on the journey is to connect deeply with yourself and discover your own mental/emotional patterns.

LOVE ON PURPOSE EXERCISES

It's time to get your journal book out and explore your motivation for a new way to "do" love. You'll begin with examining your "Why?" and then move on to explore your specific patterns that have kept you from the lasting love you desire. Having a strong "Why" will help you stay motivated through the ups and downs of your journey.

Your "Why?"

What prompted you to pick up this book and begin this journey? The answer to this question is your "Why?" Freewrite about your feelings regarding the current state of your love life, without judgment, like writing out a short story about where you are currently along with where you would like to be. Write the answers to why your past efforts haven't worked for you the way you had hoped. Include why lasting love is important to you, as well as your desires in an ideal relationship. It's best to put pen to paper (not on a digital device) and simply write from your heart without editing along the way. Set a ten-minute timer and write continuously until the timer goes off, freely expressing your thoughts and feelings about love and your past relationships. Don't worry about editing yourself or correct grammar; just get it out of your head and onto the page.

After you've completed this exercise, review your writing and without overthinking, select a number between one and ten to rate your desire to change your patterns and bust through your love blocks. One equals not very important to you, and ten equals the most important thing in your life today. Mark your score at the top of the page and put a circle around it.

Complete the Following Chart of Your Relationship History

As you chart your relationship history, include all of your significant relationships. Significant is not necessarily about the length of time; instead consider your emotional investment. A relationship that lasted only a few weeks but left you feeling devastated when it ended would fit the description of being significant. If you haven't had many relationships, you may want to include situations where you had hoped for someone to reciprocate your feelings, any person you've pined for, and make the duration about your desire. For example, perhaps you yearned for someone for two years while you were in college.

When Was the Relationship?	How Long Did It Last?	Rate Intensity (0–10)	Who Pursued Who?	How Did It End?	Who Ended It?

When Was the Relation-ship?	How Long Did It Last?	Rate Intensity (0–10)	Who Pursued Who?	How Did It End?	Who Ended It?

Discovering Your Patterns

Now it's time to discover the "You Are Here" spot on the map to your beloved. If you're at a mall you've never been to before and you want to locate a fancy luggage shop, you'd go to the directory and locate the store. On the directory, you'll find a "You Are Here" sticker. Without the "You Are Here" spot on the map, you have no idea where you are in relation to where you want to go.

This is a perfect analogy for how you've been trying to find lasting love. Knowing your patterns and strategies for love puts you in the driver's seat to create change. Answering the questions in this exercise will help determine your patterns as well as identify the negative emotions you're holding on to. Consider each question deliberately, while also being honest, kind, and compassionate with yourself. Set any judgement aside and find compassion for yourself. Let's embark on this journey together; we're committed to being your guides along the way.

1. What are your biggest fears in relationship?
2. What limiting beliefs do you have about love?
3. What are you clear that you *don't* want in relationship?
4. What are your beliefs about who you *should* be in relationship? Do you have any personal judgments, family expectations, or societal beliefs that you feel obligated to fulfill?
5. Who do you believe your partner *should* be? Do you have any personal judgments, family expectations, or societal beliefs that you believe your partner should fulfill?
6. What judgments do you have about what other people and/or society think is important in a relationship?
7. If you could revisit one moment in a past relationship and do something differently, what would it be?
8. Which one quality about yourself would you most like to change that you believe would bring you closer to the relationship you desire?
9. Which one quality in your current or past partners would you most like to change that you believe would bring you closer to the relationship you desire?

Now, looking over the chart of your relationship history along with your answers to these nine questions, what *patterns* and *repetitions* do you notice? Maybe you see a pattern of self-sacrifice or of choosing emotionally unavailable partners. Perhaps you're the person who always initiates the breakup. Take note of any patterns and repetitions you're able to spot, and make a list of them in your journal. You'll be referring to this later on in order to create the change in your love life that you desire.

Scan the QR code for bonus materials and video trainings:

2

Your Emotional Guidance System

"The best and most beautiful things in the world cannot be seen or even heard but must be felt with the heart."
—Helen Keller

Our society values intellect above emotions and feelings, but both serve a purpose so you can live a fulfilling and balanced life. Your emotional life is crucial because it acts as a compass so you can find your true North. If you're focused on your thoughts at the expense of your feelings, you're out of balance and disconnected from yourself. When you're disconnected from your emotions, you're out of rapport with yourself. To create emotional connection with another person, you must first identify and speak your feelings, and this requires you to be grounded in your body and out of your head. To connect with a partner, you must first be connected to yourself.

Unfortunately, many people have parents who discounted their emotions, either by ignoring their outbursts or telling them to just get over it. This strategy is often passed down from generation to generation, continuing the cycle of emotional disconnection and dysfunction. Additionally, many children are rewarded for swallowing their emotions and sticking with the family dynamic.

In many subtle and not-so-subtle ways throughout your life, you learned not to trust your feelings. You may even believe that it's inappropriate for you to feel certain emotions and have suppressed them (like anger). Whether your parents told you outright, "You shouldn't be upset," or they celebrated your intellect and ignored your emotional life, you were taught that emotions should be repressed, excused, or judged, and definitely not trusted. This disconnect puts you out of rapport with yourself and causes you to act against your best interests.

Being disconnected from your emotional life trips you up with recognizing the right match for you in many different ways. The following stories of two clients reveal how being disconnected from your emotional life can manifest in polar opposite strategies that block the ability to create a lasting connection.

Eva is an attractive woman who looks ten years younger than her age. Even with her beauty, she found it difficult to connect with men. They'd come on strong, but after three to four dates, they'd disappear or bow out, no longer interested in pursuing her. While she was starting to fall for them, they weren't feeling a connection and described her as a "cold blonde." She told us that she doesn't feel cold at all and didn't relate to this depiction of her personality.

Eva never knew her father and was raised by her strict German grandmother while her mother was off living her life, popping in now and again when it was convenient. Eva's grandmother didn't show much emotion and didn't allow her granddaughter to be emotionally demonstrative. If they had a disagreement, Eva's grandmother would spend days not speaking a word. Eva's strategy of clamming up when she felt strong emotions was born from fear of disconnection. It felt terrifying to her when her grandmother shut her out. Unknowingly, she'd created a surefire way to come across as detached and uninterested.

Anika grew up in a tight-knit Indian community in the South. She had a secure home life, and her parents prioritized education and finding a stable career path above everything else. Her parents weren't verbally or physically expressive, and achievement was expected and not rewarded. Throughout Anika's childhood she often heard her parents fighting, and their shouting down the hall frightened her. She fulfilled her parents' ambitions by establishing a successful career in medicine, but her personal relationships were always a mess. She would easily lose her sense of self or become overly critical. She bottled up her emotions until she couldn't handle it anymore and then exploded like a volcano. Anika's emotional life was a powerful force in her relationships, but she had no ability to considerately communicate her feelings or control them. She would eventually burst and blurt out at inappropriate times, dooming her relationships. Anika came to us to help her identify an ideal match, but she also received a masterclass in emotional intelligence and communication skills.

The word *feeling* has a double meaning as it refers to emotions as well as physical sensations in the body. It's just as common to ask, "How are you feeling?" to someone who's going through a difficult time as it is to ask, "How is your stomach feeling?" to someone who's experiencing intestinal distress. However, emotions and the physical sensations that result from them aren't separate experiences; both are signals from your subconscious mind that there's something for you to pay attention to, and both are expressed through the body. Your emotional life doesn't live in your mind; it's all physical sensations. In essence, all your emotions are body sensations and give you data regarding your experience of the present moment.

Tuning into your physical body and noticing the location and sensations you experience when angry, anxious, depressed, or excited connects you with your emotional life. This is your emotional guidance system, and mastering this connection allows you to be in the present moment, connected to yourself, and most importantly to speak your truth. If you've been conditioned your whole life to ignore these sensations or taught that your emotions are inappropriate or out of control, it may be difficult to experience them because you've been encouraged to rationalize them away. For example, Eva's grandmother punished her with silence for having emotions. She learned to hide them to the point of finding it difficult to connect with a potential partner. Anika's emotions were a storm inside of her that made it difficult for her to be vulnerable or to express love or affection. Instead, she parroted her parents' criticisms, pushing partners away.

The logical and rational part of you is responsible for evaluating and analyzing information. This part of your mind is linear, logical, and binary and is excellent at creating systems and solving problems. Your emotional life follows a different set of guidelines, one that doesn't fit the linear logic of your rational self. Instead, your emotional life can seem like a grab bag, and you never know what you'll pull out next. Think of your emotions as waves that are coming to shore. Waves come in sets and can vary in size from extra-small to extra-large, and once they crash onshore, they recede.

Your emotions are just like the waves at the beach—they vary in intensity and impact. However, your emotions aren't a problem to solve; they're not linear or logical. If you attempt to use your brain to solve your emotions, the energy is cut off at the neck, swirling around in your head with thoughts like, "What do I do with this?" over and over. We call this *blender brain*. Your brain is spinning, and you're stuck because your brain isn't the right tool to deal with your emotional life. It'd be like trying to cut your hair with a butter knife—it's great for spreading butter on toast but not great at giving you a haircut. The brain wants *to do* something with your emotions, so usually it ends up judging them. Ultimately, you're not a human doing, you're a human *being*—this is most evident with your emotions because all that's required is *to be* with your feelings by acknowledging them. Your body is meant to do more things than carry your brain around from one room to another and have sex. Plus your body is the right place for you to experience your emotions, so you can simply take note of them and then decide whether or not to take action.

In your family of origin, you may have been taught that certain emotions are bad or wrong, like anger or any kind of upset. There are no bad emotions; in fact, all of your feelings are appropriate. Your emotion is simply giving you information about yourself, just like the pain you feel when you put weight on an injured ankle is there to guide you to protect your ankle so it can heal. Only the actions you take due to your feeling state may or may not be appropriate. If you're angry at someone and you kill them, clearly that's not an acceptable action.

In some families, it's not safe to express emotion; in others, sensitivity is teased and devalued, or perhaps emotions are brushed aside while academic achievements are praised above everything else. For most of you struggling to create a lasting, loving partnership, you could have been taught that emotions should be repressed, excused, or judged, and definitely were not to be trusted. Being disconnected from your emotional life can lead you to second guess, emotionally abandon yourself, go into sacrifice, and create a habit of looking outside of yourself for validation, connection, and approval. Through our guidance, Eva started connecting to her emotional life and her intuition, and she became more aware of the subtle emotions she was experiencing. Her tendency was to downplay her emotions and to look for validation from others about her experience. The sadness and grief she felt about her failed relationships were more of an inconvenience to her. It wasn't until she started paying attention to her emotional life that all the grief and sadness about her childhood bubbled up to the surface to be healed. Her heart softened, and she felt more comfortable sharing her feelings while dating, even with guys she was just getting to know. She's now in a healthy long-term relationship with a man who feels her warmth and affection.

Anika's tendency had been to keep her desires to herself and feel frustration that her wants and needs weren't being met. Her dating life changed dramatically by learning to speak up about her goals and dreams for the future. By connecting to her feelings and expressing them, she ended a frustrating on-again/off-again relationship for good. Once free from the guy who was never a good match for her, she finally feels confident that she can find a man to create a future and a family with.

Understanding Your Emotional Stories

Your mind is a meaning-making machine, and it constantly creates a narrative from your experiences. When these narratives trigger an emotional response, we call them emotional stories. Emotional stories are the inner dialog you have with yourself about your emotional life. They're created from the desire to understand why you're experiencing certain emotions, usually feelings that are uncomfortable (what we call negative emotions).

Your emotional stories can create a scenario for why you are the way you are, therefore assigning meaning to events. Since event A happened and you felt B, that must mean that C is true. For example, Eva learned from her grandmother that her emotions weren't important. This left her feeling hurt and angry and believing that her emotions "pushed people away." When men told her she was cold, even though in her mind she'd made it clear she was interested in them, it triggered feelings of hurt and anger. These feelings of hurt and anger created another instance where her emotions pushed people away, causing her to close off even more, blocking her from showing affection and vulnerability. The meaning that Eva took from her grandmother being incapable of acknowledging her feelings was that Eva would be rejected if she expressed herself.

Anika's fear of conflict originated from listening to her parents fighting when she was a little girl. The emotional story that expressing herself would lead to conflict kept her from speaking up in her relationships. She would swallow her feelings and hope that her partner would somehow intuit what was wrong and reach out to her. The irony is that her attempts to avoid conflict with her partner actually caused a bigger rift that would ultimately end the relationship.

It's not your emotions that block you from love; it's the meaning that you've assigned to your emotions and the strategies you've adopted for dealing with them.

It's not your emotions that block you from love; it's the meaning that you've assigned to your emotions and the strategies you've adopted for dealing with them. Your emotional stories aren't based in the truth of who you are. They're limitations that you've taken on because your brain interprets circumstances by assigning meaning to your emotional experiences. There are many decisions you made about yourself long before you knew who you were and how the world works.

Your mind doesn't just slant your memory of events toward the negative; your mind can also slant circumstances toward the positive and create a fantasy from desire. For example, Susan believed in love at first sight and the magic and romance of falling in love. She was drawn to men who made declarations of love after just one or two dates. She reached out to us for help when her heart was broken by a guy who disappeared after their first conflict. Susan's mother was emotionally unstable and a narcissist, and her dad was her protector throughout her childhood. The role her father played in her upbringing aligned with her dreams of being swept off her feet, like a Disney princess. Even though she was a grown woman, a survivor of a life-threatening illness, and the CEO of her own company, when it came to love she was still dating like a teenager.

Susan had a pattern of investing emotionally in the guys who "lit her up" with romantic texts, despite the fact that they had yet to meet in person. She would talk about them as good prospects and fantasize about a future with them despite the fact that they were still complete strangers. Susan's commitment to breaking the pattern of her emotional story began with the recognition that she had an unrealistic expectation of being swept off her feet from the start. She wanted a man to make her feel special, the same way her father did. Susan was finally able to recognize her pattern of futurizing and instead slow down through the dating process and evaluate if a guy's words and actions were in alignment before she invested her heart.

The awareness that your mind can slant things toward the positive or slant things toward the negative can be used as speed bumps keeping your mind in check by focusing on facts. Past events continue to hold power over you because of the emotion attached to them, positive or negative. The plot points of the past aren't changeable. We don't have a time machine to take you back and alter past events; however, you can change the meaning that you've assigned to past experiences. In fact, you've probably had plenty of upsetting events that in hindsight and with wisdom don't have any effect on your current life. The emotions that you felt at the time didn't stick, and you were able to let it go. We would guess that since you've let go of the emotion surrounding those details, you don't even think about these events. It's not that you've forgotten these events happened; they just don't stand out for you.

There are plenty of beliefs from childhood that you're no longer invested in. Somewhere along the way you received more information, and you let go of those old beliefs. Santa Claus is a perfect example. If you were raised to believe in Santa Claus as a child, it was likely upsetting to discover it was just your parents that placed presents under the tree. Are you still upset today that Santa Claus isn't real? The truth is you were able to let go of that old belief based on new information. The same is true for all your past experiences.

By bringing awareness to your emotional stories, you can assess whether they're helpful or just an old wound that's keeping you blocked. You can't change the experiences you've had, but you can change the meaning that you give them. If your brain is spinning about something that happened to you,

> *You can't change the experiences you've had, but you can change the meaning that you give them.*

that's a negative emotional story triggering you to feel disempowered or like a victim. Troubling memories can haunt you and leave you open to re-experiencing the situation in your mind over and over again. Being able to transform your memories of troubling events puts you back in your power and connected to the present moment.

You may think that your memories are accurate recollections of past events, but in reality, your memories are colored by your emotional stories, making your recollection malleable. You can't change the plot points of the past, but you can reclaim your power by transforming your emotional connection to specific experiences. This process starts with getting in touch with your emotional guidance system. Identifying your feelings separate from your circumstances brings awareness to your emotional state. Awareness is the doorway you must walk through before transformation; first, discover your emotional guidance system and observe it like a third party, without judgment. It's important for you to discover your emotional patterns before attempting to make any changes. The exercise at the end of this chapter will give you a framework for discovering these patterns and lay the groundwork for changing them.

It's true that all your emotions are valid; however, there are some emotions people try to avoid altogether or judge themselves for having them. Part of the human experience is feeling the full range of emotions. Unfortunately, most people want to cherry-pick and only experience the feel-good emotions and avoid the rest. That's really not part of the deal here on planet Earth. In our work, we refer to the six core negative emotions—negative emotions being the ones most people attempt to avoid. They're not negative because they're somehow bad or off-limits; we call them negative because people don't like to experience them.

The six core negative emotions are fear, anger, sadness, hurt, shame, and guilt. These six emotions are at the core of your negative experiences, with other shades of emotion falling under the category of each major negative emotion. For example, frustration and irritation are lighter shades of anger, while anxiety and worry can be drilled down to fear. Embarrassment and humiliation are a form of shame, melancholy and depression are types of sadness, and upset and resentment are forms of hurt. Remorse and regret are levels of guilt. Drilling down to one of the six core negative emotions allows you to label your emotional experience quickly and easily.

The stories you tell yourself about your experiences continue to have power over you because one or more of the six core negative emotions are attached to your limiting beliefs. For example, you don't just believe that all men will cheat; you're hurt or angry about being betrayed. It's not true that all the good ones are taken, but the fear that you'll end up alone keeps this limiting belief alive. You don't just believe that love requires sacrifice; you feel guilty asking for what you want (or you worry that you don't deserve it). It's not just an assumption no one finds you attractive; you feel sad that you can't find someone to love you. You may think that you're unlovable, but it's really the shame of feeling unworthy that keeps love at bay.

Some of your limiting beliefs hold more than one of the six core negative emotions, making them particularly sticky to your subconscious mind. Negative experiences stick like Velcro in the subconscious, and positive experiences tend to slide off like Teflon. Tasked with keeping you alive, your subconscious mind can't judge or evaluate, so your emotional stories compound with your limiting beliefs, creating similar experiences over and over again. These cycles are so detrimental to your search for lasting love that you can become apathetic toward having love at all!

There are many "Law of Attraction" coaches who place emphasis on thinking positively to attract your desires into your life. However, it's not your thoughts alone that attract experiences into your life, it's the emotion attached to your thoughts that creates the rudder on your boat. We mentioned earlier that you're not *attracting* people and experiences, instead it's your subconscious highlighting familiar experiences and dynamics. This misnomer is widespread; you're not *attracting* people and particular experiences, you're *attracted to* people and certain experiences. Your beliefs are reflected back to you, shaping the way you see the world. In essence, the world appears to you as you believe it to be.

Your beliefs actually come before your experiences, not the other way around. Your emotional story about love causes you to highlight events that reinforce your beliefs. Ultimately, what you believe is true is true for you, so if you want a different outcome, you'll have to change your beliefs. Discovering the difference between the emotion you're feeling and the story attached to the feeling is the ticket to disengaging from your emotional stories and creating space to choose a different response. The wonderful thing about being human is that if you have a choice in your behavior, you will always choose the one that brings you more joy.

Identifying your feelings and labeling them can be difficult if you weren't allowed to have your emotional experiences in your family of origin. It can be easy to confuse emotions with thoughts or opinions. Allowing your cerebral cortex to lead you through life can garner a lot of goodies and can further disconnect you from your emotional guidance system. It's very common for people to spin in their heads while thinking about and analyzing emotions. This leads to judging your emotional state and wondering why you feel a particular way. Knowing why you feel the way you do will not bring you the peace of mind you're looking for. That information won't solve the puzzle or give you new strategies or behaviors. Committing to the following exercise will bring your attention to your specific mental/emotional patterns.

LOVE ON PURPOSE EXERCISE—IDENTIFY YOUR EMOTIONAL PATTERNS

You can't change something you're not aware of. The first step to reclaiming your power from your emotional stories and learning to trust your emotional guidance system is to identify your daily emotional patterns. Awareness puts you in the driver's seat to create change.

Start by setting six alarms on your phone throughout the day. Set the alarms two to three hours apart. When the alarm goes off, find a quiet place alone and take a moment to identify your current feeling state. (If you're at work, or with a group of people, you can always excuse yourself and go to the bathroom to be by yourself.) Choose a label, ideally a one-word emotion, or if you're unable to label how you feel emotionally, describe your physical sensations and the location of the sensations in your body. Remember, emotions are body sensations, so if you're having difficulty labeling your feelings, start with physical sensations, for example, *I feel anxious*, or *I feel a tightness in my stomach, like a knot.*

Track your emotions daily, writing them down in your journal using a chart like the one that follows. (You can also create something in your smartphone or tablet to track your emotions over a few weeks.) Note the time of day for each alarm, and then track your feeling state when each alarm goes off for a particular day of the week. Do this for three to four weeks so you have time to discover your emotional patterns.

Some of your emotions are circumstantial, and it's easy to trace them to an event. Other emotions seem to appear out of thin air, just free-flowing emotions that come and go. Set judgment aside throughout this entire process. Track your emotions like a third-party observer who's simply collecting facts. Judgment will impede the process and leave you feeling bad. Instead, focus on what's true for you in the moment so you can discover your emotional patterns. After a week or two, see if you can discern your emotional patterns. Your awareness of them must come before any change can occur. In Part II, Transformation, you'll string these concepts together to create lasting change.

	Sunday	Monday	Tuesday	Wednesday	Thursday	Friday	Saturday
Alarm 1:							
Alarm 2:							
Alarm 3:							
Alarm 4:							
Alarm 5:							
Alarm 6:							

Scan the QR code for bonus materials and video trainings:

3

What Are You Saying to Yourself About Yourself?

"Change your thoughts if you wish to change your circumstances. Since you alone are responsible for your thoughts, only you can change them."

—*Paramhansa Yogananda*

Becoming a wildly successful businesswoman who built an empire in an arena previously dominated by men is only one of the accomplishments of our client Maureen. Her business success meant she didn't have to worry about finances, which allowed her to be very generous with family and friends. We noticed that Maureen was extremely hard on herself. Her inner critic was constantly beating herself up for one thing or another. She didn't understand us when we'd tell her she had an unrealistic expectation of herself, that she expected to be superhuman, and that she needed to love and accept herself as is. She'd tell us, "I buy myself anything I want, so I'm not sure what you mean." In her mind the fact that she bought herself material things meant that she loved herself.

One day Maureen shared with us that a couple days prior, while waiting to make a left turn, she saw a homeless man holding a sign for help in the center median. Pulling up next to him, she gave him $20 and driving away the voice in her head said, "You're so cheap! You could have given him a lot more money than that! What's wrong with you?!" Finally hearing her brutal inner dialog, Maureen was overcome with emotion, pulled the car over, and burst into tears. All of our insights fell into place as she realized she was constantly berating herself, falling short of her unrealistic expectation that she would solve everyone's problems (even strangers begging for money).

The most important relationship you'll ever have is the one you have with yourself.

The most important relationship you'll ever have is the one you have with yourself. How you speak to yourself informs you of the state of that relationship. The problem is most people are like Maureen, completely unaware that they have an inner dialog. In this case, ignorance is *not* bliss because being unaware leaves you susceptible to your subconscious habits of thought. There are three things in life that you have control over—what you think, feel, and do. It may not feel like you have control over your thoughts since they seem to just pop into your mind without prompting; however, your random thoughts are actually habits, and with concentration and awareness you can release habits that no longer serve you and create new habits that are useful to you. The realization that you can take control of your thoughts, feelings, and actions can empower you to dramatically change your life for the better. You have a choice in how you think about your circumstances. You have a choice in how you feel about events in your life. And you have a choice in the actions you take in response to your thoughts and feelings. This is your gateway to freedom and allows you to create a life you love.

Becoming aware of your inner dialog allows you to identify the chronic thoughts that leave you feeling unworthy, insecure, frustrated, and afraid (just to name a few). Despite Maureen's business success, she was unhappy in her life, constantly striving to do more. Her negative thoughts were not a conscious choice; they were cobbled together when she was a little girl in her family of origin. She criticized herself for not doing enough, for not being good enough to deserve the love she desired. Her inner critic would constantly tell her, "Who would marry you? You need to work on yourself!" The mental strategies that were the foundation for Maureen's success in business had her behaving like a doormat in her personal relationships. Once the trance was broken that day driving her car, she would never be able to tune out her inner critic again (and it was just a matter of time before she changed those negative thoughts to positive ones).

The awareness of your inner critic is an essential step on the journey to your beloved. Once you're in an intimate relationship, your partner becomes like a fun-house mirror, and it can be difficult to see that the distorted reflection is filled with your wounds, frustrations, and inner criticisms mirrored back at you. Psychologists call this phenomenon "projecting," a defense mechanism for coping with stress by assigning your thoughts, feelings, and behaviors onto another person. If you're unaware of your inner dialog, it's easy to project your negative self-talk onto your partner. But when you upgrade your inner dialog, you're more resourceful and better able to identify an ideal match rather than select your familiar family dynamic.

Your inner dialog is shaped by your childhood experiences, your limiting beliefs, and your level of self-esteem. By the time you're an adult searching for love, your inner dialog is an unconscious habit. Tuning in to the voice inside your head shines a spotlight on your belief system. Your thoughts shape your experience of the events in your life; they influence how you interpret what's happening, the meanings you assign to those events, and how you feel about them. The world appears to you as you believe it to be, and it's your inner dialog that reveals those beliefs to you (some of your beliefs are helpful, and some prevent you from doing things you're capable of and desire to do).

In her thirties, Orna delved deeper into healing her childhood trauma and discovered that her inner critic had an Eastern European dialect—just like her mother. She was hard on herself in every way her mother was, mocking her and belittling her, and no matter her achievements they were never enough. She had internalized her mother's voice and had confused it as her own for decades. Does your inner critic stem from a parent or authority figure in your life? Does it echo your insecurities or stem from low self-esteem? Or is it your own guilt, fear, or shame speaking to you?

At first, it can be difficult to identify your inner critic, especially if you're not aware that you're talking to yourself. You may believe you don't have an inner dialog. It may not show up as a voice in your head; perhaps it's a recurring thought or a knee-jerk reaction in certain situations. Maybe you find yourself constantly inferring criticism from other's comments, or you could be walking on eggshells waiting for the other shoe to drop. Beware of time travel! Like Matthew, you could be making things up about the future, or perhaps you're regularly triggered by past events like Orna, or a myriad of other options. Notice if you're making things up about someone else's behavior or making assumptions, and most importantly look for patterns. You can discover your inner dialog by either hearing it for the first time or by simply seeing the effects of it on your behavior.

Another way to discover your inner voice is to start with your feelings and look for the meaning you've attached to your emotions. As we discussed in Chapter Two, your feelings are simply subconscious signals. The meanings you've assigned to your feelings reveal the thoughts and beliefs that are the catalyst for your emotional life.

This is what we call the *think–feel–do* cycle. You have a thought, and that thought triggers a feeling, and that feeling is the catalyst for a behavior that doesn't serve you. You can identify your pattern by starting with your emotions and then working backward. For example, you're feeling upset about a particular situation in your life and you're unhappy with how you handled it. Start by identifying the triggering emotion and notice how it affected your behavior. You may have felt you had no choice in how you reacted. Digging deeper beyond the emotion, see if you can identify the meaning you're assigning to the event. What does it mean about you? Now you've identified the thought that triggered your emotional reaction.

The realization that your thoughts shape your reality should give you pause to examine which thoughts are causing you pain and loneliness in your love life. Often, how you're thinking about the problem is the problem. For example, if you're struggling with finding dates on a dating app and you believe that dating apps don't work and you're wasting your time because there aren't any good matches on apps, then you'll quickly grow tired of using a dating app. However, dating research will tell you that more people are meeting their spouse on dating apps than at any time in history (70 percent success rate, according to *Forbes* magazine). If you change your beliefs about what is possible for you, then you can change your results. It's helpful to question all of your beliefs and see if they're worth keeping around. Any belief that leaves you feeling unempowered or feeling like a victim isn't serving you or helping you to get the love you want. Ultimately, suffering is optional, and taking an inventory of your beliefs and your habitual thoughts is the foundation for creating a happier more fulfilling life.

In *The System of Doctor Tarr and Professor Fether*, Edgar Allen Poe says, "Don't believe everything you think." And yet many people are slaves to their limiting beliefs about love and dating. They don't take responsibility for their thoughts about dating, which trigger negative feelings about whether dating is worth it. Maybe they believe it's a waste of time, creating feelings of apathy so they take no actions at all, or they end up feeling overwhelmed and stuck in analysis paralysis. Accepting responsibility for your thoughts means that you're the only one with the power to change them. Stop looking for outside evidence to change your beliefs. Instead, change your beliefs, and the evidence you see will support your new belief system. Throughout your journey, sticking with the exercises will support this change to occur over time; it won't be instantaneous. Instead of being a slave to your thoughts, stop giving them so much power over you. Most random thoughts that you have during the day appear because of habit. You've trained your mind to fill in the empty space with a set of usual thoughts. You may be wondering why you keep having certain repetitive thoughts. Our answer is because you've created a habit of thinking that way. The best part is once you're aware of your habitual thought patterns, you can change them.

The most essential ingredient to identifying your patterns is to stay out of judgment so you can simply see what is occurring. Judging yourself for *what is* will simply keep you stuck in your current think–feel–do cycle. Pause as many times as you need to and find compassion for yourself through the process. Like peeling an onion, you're going back through layers of habit to discover the limiting belief that is setting off your cycle. To create the change you're looking for, sit in the seat of the observer and notice *what is* without judgment. This practice will also serve you when you're sharing your life with a partner because that person will be imperfect, and you'll have miscommunication and conflict with your beloved. Practicing kindness and compassion with yourself will pay off in spades when you're with your soulmate.

People are complicated, so you may have more than one emotion at a time. Even your negative emotions will compound. You can feel one way at an event, and you may have a completely different feeling about the person you are attending the event with. Drilling down through your unique think–feel–do cycle is the first step to becoming a master of your emotional life. All human beings get triggered; it's a normal occurrence. The best you can do is recognize as quickly as possible that you're triggered and then work to calm your nervous system. On this journey, you'll receive tips and many tools to practice for this purpose.

If you're just waiting for circumstances in your life to magically change, whether it's your feelings, your results, or your relationship status, you'll be waiting forever. The only person who can change your life is you. Take charge of your feeling state by identifying your inner dialog and breaking your negative mental/emotional habits. By taking conscious inventory of your inner dialog, you can alter your negative thoughts and change them to positive ones. Transform your inner experience, and your outer world will change.

As Matthew sobered up in his early thirties, he began shifting his beliefs and behaviors that triggered him into feeling bad about himself. One of the reasons Matthew sought escape through drugs and alcohol was that back then he didn't like himself, and it was the best way to numb his feelings of self-hatred. Early in his sobriety, he had the realization that he was solely responsible for his own happiness. One morning in the shower getting ready for work, Matthew started imagining an argument with his boss, and he spent several minutes quarreling in his mind over a situation that hadn't happened yet. He was upset over something that wasn't even real. If he had continued down this path, once at work it would've been easy for him to overreact, get defensive, and create the argument he had imagined in the shower.

At that moment, Matthew burst out laughing! Realizing that he got triggered over an imagined clash, he couldn't stop himself laughing uncontrollably in the shower. Collecting himself, he took action right away to counteract his habit of negative self-talk. Out loud in the shower he said, "That's not true! I'm making this up! It didn't happen!" Coming into the present moment, Matthew took control of his thoughts, finished showering, and with a smile on his face went to work without the usual anticipation of conflict. By interrupting the tendency to be on the defensive, he was free to enjoy his day without any conflicts, real or imagined.

Do you fear others criticizing you? Are you worried you'll upset someone if you speak your truth? Are you constantly imagining bad things happening to you? No matter your negative mental/emotional patterns, begin by identifying your inner dialog and self-limiting beliefs. Once you're able to recognize them, you're in the driver's seat to make the necessary changes to improve your life and experience more joy.

Changing Your Inner Dialogue

A paper tiger may look powerful and scary, but the threat isn't real. Just like a paper tiger, your emotional fears can't hurt you;

there's no physical danger. You won't even break a nail; there's literally no chance of physical harm. To create change, the goal is to make fear your friend. If you're walking down the street and you see a friend in the distance, you'd go toward your friend, not try to run away from them. Creating a practice of leaning into actions that scare you can only change your life for the better. Who you are at your highest and best self is not visible to you, because that version of you lives in your blind spot. There's a force-field around the path to your highest and best self, and that force-field is made up of fear. You connect with your beloved on the path to your highest and best self.

In the body, the physical manifestations of fear and excitement are the same. Your heart rate increases, your breath becomes shallow, and your palms may get sweaty; the only difference between fear and excitement is your inner dialog. The same physical sensations can have completely different meanings depending on what you're saying to yourself about what is occurring. Imagine you're in line waiting to board a rollercoaster. You could be saying to yourself, "This is going to be so much fun! I can't wait!" or "I can't believe I'm getting on that rollercoaster! Where's the chicken exit!" Either way, your body is reacting the same way; the only difference is your inner dialogue and therefore your perception of the events.

When you let your fears control you, you react to mundane events as if they are life-threatening. You react to emotional fears the same way you'd react to being chased by a real tiger. Your fear stories trigger your fight/flight/freeze response, and you take action to keep yourself safe. But having a bad date isn't a life-threatening event. You're not going to die because a person you like doesn't like you back. It may not feel great, but you'll survive, and when you're able to face those fears, your confidence will grow. Your emotional fears about love and dating aren't keeping you safe from danger; they're preventing you from growing and becoming more resilient. Developing resiliency will serve you in every part of your life, including your search for lasting love. Take note of your emotional stories that trigger your fears and keep you stuck.

You may discover that fear has paralyzed your love life and that your mental/emotional patterns are based in fear—fear of rejection, fear of conflict, fear of saying or doing the wrong thing—but your fear-invoking thoughts are just "paper tigers." Your fears about love and dating are not life-threatening. We don't mean to diminish your experiences or your feelings; your trials and tribulations happened to you. However, the meaning you've given to these ordeals could be triggering your emotional fears and keeping you from taking action, or even worse, causing you to take actions that lead to self-sabotage.

Changing your negative, fear-inducing thoughts to more positive and empowering thoughts will create motivation rather than suck your energy dry. When you regularly think empowering, positive thoughts, you'll feel more confident dating, you won't see every hiccup as if you're doomed, and you'll be more willing to take risks and have the uncomfortable conversations necessary to discover if someone is your match. Don't allow the paper tiger of fear to block you from having a lasting, loving partnership. Become a master of your inner voice and empower yourself to make your dream life a reality.

Isabel was constantly afraid she was going to make a mistake. Having grown up with an extremely critical father, she felt she had to be perfect to earn his love. She was constantly second guessing herself, overthinking every decision she had to make. Isabel believed no one would ever love her unconditionally, and when she met an attractive man, her first thought was, "He would never be interested in me." The only men she found attractive were the ones who didn't give her the time of day, and the ones who would approach her or reach out online she would reject outright. Stuck in this frustrating cycle of rejection, she finally reached out to us. Identifying her fear story and bringing it to her attention revealed her internal pattern of judgment. All day every day, she judged herself and others.

Isabel had internalized her father's criticism to mean she had to live by an unrealistic standard of perfection. First, we shifted her inner dialog to, "I can be loved for my humanness. I am loved no matter what." Rather quickly, she saw results and her mind began to highlight events where it was okay to make a mistake, and where she was accepted even when imperfect. We asked her to celebrate and cement these experiences at the end of the day when they occurred. As Isabel became less rigid and critical of herself and others, she started having more experiences of feeling accepted and safe. Her heart opened like a flower in bloom, and like never before, men came out of the woodwork. She came into session singing, "It's raining men! Hallelujah!" Her dating calendar filled up, and she finally had options to choose a good match. Rather than repeating her cycle of judgment and rejection, she started experiencing opportunities that had always been available to her.

These opportunities weren't visible to Isabel before due to a negative hallucination. A hallucination is seeing something that's not there, and a negative hallucination is not seeing something that is right in front of you. This is the power of your mindset and inner dialog. If you imagine wonderful, miraculous things happening to you all the time, they will. If you imagine that everything will create more misery, you may feel cursed because nothing goes your way. You may have built up walls around your heart like Isabel because your fears have fooled you into believing that love isn't safe. Ultimately, these walls are keeping you from the thing you want most of all—lasting love with an ideal partner. Face your paper tigers, walk through them, and you'll discover that they're not real! Managing your mindset and mastering your inner dialog doesn't mean you'll never have a bad day; it just means that one bad day won't create a month or a lifetime of agony. As you embrace new expectations for yourself, your confidence will expand and your outer world will shift to create more joyous experiences.

Isabel's new inner dialogue of "I can be loved for my humanness. I am loved no matter what," is also an affirmation. Affirmations are not a new concept; they've been an integral part of the personal development world for decades. They've even been satirized on *Saturday Night Live* with Stuart Smalley poking fun at affirmations by declaring, "I'm good enough. I'm smart enough, and doggone it, people like me!" Their ubiquity doesn't diminish their effectiveness. You've been affirming your reality whether or not you're doing it intentionally. If you say, "I can't believe I just did that! I'm such an idiot!" you'd be saying a negative affirmation about yourself. You're talking to yourself all day every day and creating your reality with your inner dialog, so you might as well affirm something positive and useful while being kind and compassionate with yourself. Give it a try! You have nothing to lose except your anxiety, loneliness, and heartache.

Changing the way you speak to yourself about yourself will transform your experiences from the inside out.

It may feel awkward at first, but changing the way you speak to yourself about yourself will transform your experiences from the inside out. Transforming your mental/emotional patterns requires consistency and commit-ment. It's more important to make small, consistent efforts than to try and change everything about your inner dialog all at once. Affirmations can shift your mindset from negative, self-doubting thoughts to more positive and empowering ones. By repeating affirmations, you're taking control of your inner dialog so you can reinforce positive beliefs about yourself and your abilities. By mastering your inner dialog with affirmations, your confidence will grow from the inside out, and over time, with consistency, you'll reap the fruits of your labor.

In order to create a potent affirmation, state everything in the positive. Next, write or say your affirmations as if they're happen-ing right now in the present moment. Don't affirm something occurring in the future; you'll just be creating more hoping and wishing. For example, "I want to meet a life partner who respects and values me," affirms the *wanting* instead of already having it. Instead, affirm it as if it is already happening like, "I feel respected and valued by the people I date."

Sometimes you'll want to affirm large goals that may feel out of reach to your current circumstances. If you are affirming some-thing that is a big change in your life, your subconscious may reject the affirmation because it just doesn't feel possible or true. Instead of focusing on goals that are a drastic change to your life, affirm that you're in the process of changing. Use language like, "I'm learning to love and value myself in all my relationships," or "I'm developing new skills to find my voice when I'm triggered." Embrac-ing in-process language when crafting an affirmation will allow your mind to accept the changes taking place.

Adding emotion to your affirmations will supercharge them for you. Another way to energize your affirmations is to turn them into a song. In musical theatre, a character will burst into song because their emotions are too potent to simply speak the words. Singing holds a high emotional vibration, and by turning your affirmations into songs you increase their emotional power and therefore their effectiveness. Your unconscious critical inner dialog is so effective at keeping you stuck because it's charged with negative emotions. With positive affirmations you can create a new habit, one where you speak to yourself with empowering emotions the way you'd like your beloved to speak to you—with compassion and kindness. You'll practice writing your own affirmations in the exercise at the end of this chapter (page 53).

Orna transformed her life by creating a song with the affirmation, "I love and approve and accept myself." The year she was training for her first triathlon, she spent many hours each week singing this affirmation while swimming, biking, and running. All of these seemingly miraculous things occurred in her life. It wasn't until later when she looked back to discover the catalyst for a series of serendipitous events that she realized it was this one new habit that changed her circumstances dramatically for the better. Because this habit was created during physical activity, at one point it dawned on Orna that she starts singing this affirmation whenever she's engaged in physical activity. It's not a choice she's making because it's become an unconscious habit. She's also used it to feel good about herself in situations that she knows will activate her inner critic.

Over a decade ago, we were at a hotel in Las Vegas for a media training. As we headed down the long hallway to the suite for our workshop, Orna started singing this affirmation quietly so Matthew could hear.

Matthew asked, "Baby, are you not feeling good about yourself today?"

Orna replied, "No, I just know that when I see myself on camera later I can be super critical of my appearance, so I'm setting myself up now to only say nice things to myself no matter what."

Thirteen out of fourteen producers booked us for a media appearance that day. Speaking kindly to yourself pays off in more ways than you can imagine. All we ask is that you run the experiment yourself. Commit to the Love on Purpose Exercise with affirmations at the end of this chapter. This is our coaches' challenge for you: Play full out and put in one hundred percent effort, and we can assure you that you'll see results, more than you can even imagine right now. Your life doesn't change overnight, but over time with consistent effort you'll find that events that would normally unhinge you don't land with the same intensity, and that new opportunities and serendipity come your way more often and with regularity.

When you put all the parts together, affirming positive beliefs (think) that trigger good feelings (feel) and motivate you to take effective actions (do), you'll tap into the engine of manifestation. However, manifestation isn't a magical process that happens just because of positive thinking. A common piece of advice is to fake it until you make it or to put on a coat of confidence as if just thinking positively is all you need. Instead, manifestation occurs when you use positive thoughts to increase your enthusiasm and confidence and take that energy and momentum into your actions. This grows your self-esteem and self-confidence from the inside out.

Here's one way to increase your ability to manifest: Consciously look for evidence of your new beliefs to cement them as true. You have plenty of evidence for your negative beliefs because they've been a habit for so long. Because your mind is tasked with keeping you safe from danger, it will highlight any threat, including negative experiences, and therefore it reinforces your limiting beliefs. Now that you know that emotional dangers are just paper tigers and won't cause physical harm, you'll need evidence to support this new way of thinking. Look for evidence of love all around you, from your pet, friends, family, or approval at work. If you believe that you aren't attractive enough to be loved, take note of couples you see in the world; they are comprised of all shapes and sizes. Say to yourself, "See, if they can find love, so can I!" Find proof in the world that there's a lid for every pot.

You can find evidence of anything you want to believe about yourself. When people around you get into an exclusive relationship, send you a save-the-date for their wedding, or get engaged, decide that these events are coming closer and closer to you. Decide that you are next! Celebrate love in all its forms, and take note of couples that hold hands while they walk, or young people out on a date. Love is not like pie where someone else can take your slice—love is limitless! The awareness of your inner dialog is most important in what you say to yourself about yourself. You have one hundred percent control over how you feel about yourself and what you say about yourself, so choose your words wisely. Changing your negative thoughts to positive ones may be something you do for the rest of your life, and if your life is better in countless ways, wouldn't it be worth it?

LOVE ON PURPOSE EXERCISES

The exercise from the previous chapter of setting alarms to discover your emotional patterns lays the groundwork so you can dig deeper into your subconscious thought patterns. The first exercise will help you identify your mental/emotional patterns to gain clarity about your specific hidden blocks to love. This exercise will continue to build from that productive exercise in Chapter Two.

The second exercise in this chapter will help empower you to overcome those negative patterns that you've unearthed and create a new, more useful inner dialog.

Mental/Emotional Patterns

Examine the list of recurring negative emotions that you discovered by setting daily alarms in Chapter Two. Using your journal entries as a prompt, see if you can discover the underlying thoughts that are triggering those negative emotions. For example, if you're anxious for much of the day, you may discover that your inner dialog is about being behind and you have so much to do. If you're affirming that you're in overwhelm, it would make sense that those thoughts would trigger anxiety (a light form of fear). It can be difficult to discern your inner dialog since it's an unconscious habit, but the more you examine what thoughts may be triggering your negative emotional patterns, the more insight you'll gain.

Looking over your list of negative emotions, identify from the list of negative emotions the one you feel most frequently. Then create a list of all the thoughts that trigger it. Then move to the second most frequent negative emotion from your list and do the same thing: write out all the thoughts that trigger it, and so on down through the remaining emotions. As always, move through this exercise with love and compassion, as an observer without judgment. If you find yourself being critical (or analyzing yourself), you can borrow Orna's affirmation and take a break while saying, "I love and approve and accept myself!" (If you take this break, try saying the affirmation for a minimum of three times while throwing your hands high in the air for emphasis.)

Take note of your unhelpful thoughts and the emotions they trigger as we'll guide you to transform them in Chapter Five. If you're wondering how long you have to monitor your inner dialogue and change your negative thoughts to positive ones before you can stop (or find your beloved), that's not the right question. Instead, commit to these practices so that you can create a new lifelong pattern of positive and empowering thoughts. You don't wonder why you need to sleep, or eat, or rest, right? You know these things are necessary. Managing your mindset and your inner dialog is essential to living your best life.

Two Journal Books

When you write with a pen on paper, you're not just expressing your thoughts and feelings, you're also subconsciously revealing aspects of your personality. The way you form letters and words is an expression of your subconscious mind, which doesn't occur when typing on an electronic device. In fact, handwriting analysis is an accepted diagnostic tool in a court of law and hiring practices because handwriting has been proven to be an expression of the subconscious mind that reveals specific character traits and behaviors. Therefore, when you put pen to paper, you are also in direct communication with your subconscious. For this exercise you'll need two separate journal books. You'll want to write on paper for it to be effective.

1. In one journal book, write out your lifetime achievements. Begin this book with simple milestones from when you were a baby. Be sure to include walking and talking, as those are your first big achievements (unless you were born with a health condition or physical impairment). From there, please list all of your age-appropriate achievements—all awards, accolades, trophies, honors, ribbons, medals, add anything you're proud of. Write in this book on the days you're feeling good about yourself and read from it on the days you're feeling down. This isn't something you'll finish in one sitting. Revisit it on a regular basis to update it. Once you think the list is complete, ask a few people

in your inner circle who have known you a long time about your achievements and see if you've forgotten anything. Creating this list of lifetime achievements helps you realize that you have accomplished quite a bit in your life and you have the where-withal to create anything you desire, including lasting love.

2. In the second journal book, you're going to master your mind-set and your inner dialog before you turn out the light to go to sleep. This practice can be life-changing. Creating this new bedtime ritual will gradually transform countless areas of your life including your health, your career, and your intimate rela-tionships. Begin a nightly practice of writing down the following in this journal book longhand, so if you learned cursive writing, use that; otherwise, just write however you usually do with pen to paper (not a digital device as we explained previously):

    a. **Five successes for the day.** These can be literally right off your to-do list; they're not lifetime achievements but rather simply things you got done. If you're home sick with a cold, making toast and tea can go on this list. If you did the laun-dry that day, you can put that on the list too. If you had an extraordinary day and achieved something worthy of a life-time achievement, you would put it in both journal books. The key is to end your day on a positive note, logging all that you've accomplished.

    b. **Three affirmations three times each.** Choose your affirma-tions with the intention that these new beliefs will help you transition from where you are to where you'd like to be. You can utilize the unhelpful thoughts you've discovered that trigger negative emotions and rewrite them in the positive to make them more empowering. You can also use affirma-tions you found in a book or affirmation card deck, or you can create a new affirmation from scratch. Work with the same three affirmations for a long period of time (months to years). Once you feel like an affirmation has become a habit and you find yourself saying it to yourself unconsciously throughout the day, then you can switch it up and create new affirmations for other areas of your life. You'll write the first one three times, then the second three times, then the third three times.

c. **Five things you're grateful for.** A practice of gratitude all on its own is an effective way to change your life for the better. Make this the last thing you'll do before turning out the light to go to sleep. These can be anything: people you love, pets, qualities you admire about yourself, your vehicle (and that it gets you from point A to point B and back to A again), your home, the weather—literally anything that you truly have gratitude for in your life currently. You can change all five things every night, or you can stick with a few that remain the same and switch up others. There's no wrong way to do this; simply focus on a feeling of gratitude as you write out each item. This is a nightly celebration of all that you cherish in your life, so enjoy it!

Scan the QR code for bonus materials and video trainings:

4

Your Love Imprint

"Your task is not to seek for love, but merely to seek and find all the barriers within yourself that you have built against it."

—*Rumi*

Behind your mental/emotional patterns that we explored in the previous chapters, there is a hidden program that's driving your behavior in love. It is the original source of your limiting beliefs and the core wound behind your emotional stories. The settings of your internal love map have been the driving force behind who you find attractive and how you approach love and relationship. Your internal GPS for love has been the guiding force for who you find attractive, and if you've struggled to create long-lasting love, then those settings are corrupted. No amount of effort into an online profile or changing your dating strategies will impact your outcome. You must get to the root cause of the issue and reprogram those coordinates to reach your desired destination—your soulmate.

When you were very young, long before you knew who you were or how the world worked, you made a decision about love. This decision set the course for your journey of seeking love, approval, and acceptance. We call this decision Your Love Imprint.

It's the gap between how you wanted to be loved and your parents' (or whoever were your primary caregivers) capacity to love you. It's how you learned to receive love in your family of origin. Your Love Imprint is your core wound from childhood made up of your limiting beliefs, your mental/emotional patterns, and your behavioral strategies for giving and receiving love. It's like your own personal GPS for love guiding your behavior and every choice you make in your intimate relationships.

Your Love Imprint is your core wound from childhood made up of your limiting beliefs, your mental/emotional patterns, and your behavioral strategies for giving and receiving love.

Newborn babies are born without blocks to love. They give love freely and receive love freely from anyone willing to share it. You could say that a newborn is the physical embodiment of the energy of love. No newborn child believes that they need to prove their value or please others in order to receive love. However, as babies grow they begin to learn that love is conditional in some way.

Newborns have two emotional needs that must be fulfilled in order to survive in the world: to feel loved and to feel safe. You would do anything to ensure that you feel these two emotions, even if it means taking on limiting beliefs about yourself. We call this twisting into a pretzel to earn love. You spend much of your childhood attempting to determine just what shape will be most pleasing to your parents, allowing you to feel loved and safe. You try on different behaviors and strategies until you're all twisted up. The infant who embodied unconditional love is lost in a tangle of unsuccessful attempts to get your needs met.

Your place in birth order, whether you had siblings or come from a blended family, even extended family members may all play a role in the family system that created Your Love Imprint. This is part of the process of growing up. As you grow, you quickly discover that you must behave a certain way to get the love that you need. Maybe your father only expressed his love when you swallowed your emotions and didn't express your feelings. Or your mom rewarded you for helping her around the house with chores or when you got good grades. Sometimes you learn that to get your parents' attention you have to throw a fit and be the loudest one in the room. These requirements to receive love are not spoken aloud; they are crafted over time in a family dynamic.

Children often take full responsibility for their parents' behavior. When your parents argued with each other, were angry with you, or treated you inappropriately or carelessly, you didn't have the awareness as a child to think they lacked parenting skills. Instead, you internalized their behavior, thinking, "What's wrong with me that my parent is behaving this way?" Then you looked for evidence of that new belief. Because your sensory experience takes in a massive amount of information, you found the evidence you needed. You assigned a meaning to those events and believed that the meaning you assigned was the truth about you. You took responsibility for your parents' inability to love you the way you desired to be loved, and in doing so you took on a core wound that is running your love life. Your Love Imprint even determines who you find attractive!

None of this is meant to indict your parents or to blame them for the way you were raised. Your parents did their best—even if their best was severely limited. And they learned from their parents, and on back through the generations. This is the human condition: Many people are not loved exactly how they want to be loved in their family. The job of parenting and raising a child is the toughest one there is, and it's an imbalanced relationship. You may have had an effect on your mother and father, but their fingerprints are all over you. The decisions you made about yourself from interactions with them are written on the hard drive of your subconscious mind.

Your subconscious mind is taxed with keeping you alive, and one of its strategies is to create a physical and behavioral homeostasis—to keep things the same, or within a narrow range. Your physical homeostasis includes your heart rate, your blood pressure, and your body temperature. Your behavioral homeostasis includes your habits, your strategies, your persistent thoughts, and your emotional reactions. The subconscious mind immediately evaluates information and identifies where there's a similarity to your previous experiences. Then your mind clumps similarities together (like organizing filing cabinets or the folders on your computer's hard drive). This cataloging of information is known as the Law of Association. Your mind evaluates the information and quickly determines, "This is like that," and in doing so, it triggers your habitual response for dealing with similar situations.

The Law of Association is an important and useful tool for survival. Without it, you'd have to consciously evaluate millions of bits of information in order to make a conclusion or take an action. This would take too long and be so cumbersome that you'd never be able to decide quickly enough to get anything done. You'd be frozen by overwhelm. The habitual response is activated before you're able to make a conscious choice, circumventing your free will. Your emotional stories are the foundation of these habitual responses, so your beliefs about yourself and your circumstances are recreated. In most cases, your reaction to events is not hysterical, it's historical, meaning your emotions compound and you're responding with the weight of all the times you've been triggered into a particular emotional story.

Your Love Imprint is the operating system that looks at a potential partner and says, "This is like that." You mistake the bells and whistles going off as attraction and a soul connection, but they're actually your subconscious mind telling you, "This is familiar! This is a match to what you've already experienced!" The flaw in the system is that your subconscious mind can't judge; that happens in the cerebral cortex. You have no way of knowing if the familiar will bring you joy or sorrow; the signal is just a match to what you've already experienced. What if your desires in love are not a match to your childhood experience of love?

The choices you've been making to select a life partner have come from a blueprint you created when you were a small child. For example, we determined Bradley's love imprint as "love equals chaos." A divorced thirty-eight-year-old salesman, Bradley reached out to us because he was tired of meaningless sexual encounters and was finally ready to look at his issues with love and intimacy. His parents divorced when he was nine years old after fighting constantly in their marriage. His father was an alcoholic with anger issues. His mother lacked appropriate boundaries, often sharing intimate, emotional conversations with Bradley in her bedroom. Bradley met a woman in his early twenties, and they immediately moved in together and married within three months. She was not a good match; she regularly belittled him and repeatedly cheated on him, and they went through a bitter divorce. Since the divorce, he has struggled to make an emotional connection with any woman he dates and believes that love and sex are a minefield. Love feels chaotic and untrustworthy to Bradley. He is attracted to drama and is uncomfortable with stable, healthy relationships.

Bradley wasn't even sure he wanted a relationship. He just knew that he needed to heal the wounds of his divorce, and he was finally ready to work on his relationships with women, which were fraught with drama. He would consistently rush into relationships with women he'd just met, often moving in together after knowing them for only a few weeks. Each of these women quickly revealed a propensity for drama, and Bradley was caught in a pattern of chaos again and again. His love imprint, "love equals chaos," would highlight these women and send his subconscious the signal, "This is familiar! This is familiar!" and he would mistake the signal for attraction. Having the knowledge of his love imprint didn't initially change his behavior or dating strategies. It wasn't until Bradley was burned by three different women within a year that he finally admitted that his way of selecting a partner wasn't going to bring him the lasting connection he desired. His fear of rejection was an emotional story that would drive him to commit too quickly because it was an old familiar feeling.

Bradley's journey shows how Your Love Imprint keeps you stuck in the same heartbreaking relationship pattern over and over again. It's a "false positive" highlighting the person who energetically matches your core wound from childhood, and you mistake this signal as attraction and excitement. Your Love Imprint determines who you find attractive, and all too often those people are contrary to the person you desire to partner with. For example, you may want a partner who communicates, who is faithful, and who loves you unconditionally. However, your subconscious keeps highlighting uncommunicative cheaters who don't value you.

So why is it so difficult to change this pattern even when you recognize it? The problem is that you're likely unaware of how you determine who's attractive to you in the first place. You may have bought into the myth that lasting love will magically happen when you meet the "right" person, a special person who will love you no matter what. When you buy into this myth, you ignore what's genuinely motivating your selection process. The reason you're attracted to someone has nothing to do with your "type"; it has everything to do with recreating a pattern that you learned in childhood that was built inside your family dynamic. For some people, the issue is that your parents were great and no one can measure up. The majority of people are at the other end of the spectrum, and it's the belief that you have to somehow earn love from a parent in some way, or to the extreme—the belief that you are unlovable. In reality, you were dealt a bad hand. You simply learned a strategy for love in your family of origin that no longer serves you.

Kate's love imprint is "I can't trust love." A forty-five-year-old divorcee, she reached out to us when her three children were in their teens because she was ready to start dating again. Her ex-husband was a verbally abusive alcoholic who had her walking on eggshells in their relationship, always afraid she would set him off. A successful entrepreneur with a strong personality, Kate was afraid she wouldn't meet anyone suitable in her small Texas town. She was someone who was always striving to be a better person and couldn't understand why she couldn't find a match.

Her childhood was idyllic on the outside. With two loving parents, Kate and her older sister never lacked for getting their needs met. However, inside the house was very different from what the neighbors saw. Her father drank, had affairs, and would verbally berate her mother. Her mother was insecure and unable to stand up to him, so she put her focus on her girls. Kate swore she would never marry a man like her dad and that she would not be a doormat. Unfortunately, that's what she created with her ex-husband. When he would yell, she would close off and shut down to avoid conflict. She couldn't believe she had re-created her parents' dynamic.

Kate couldn't trust herself to choose good dating prospects, either. In the years after her divorce, she ping-ponged between two different types of men. She would date the nice guys hoping that a spark would develop between them, but the relationships would never go anywhere. Then she would have torrid affairs with emotionally unavailable men. These men would pop in and out of her life, keeping her feeling anxious and yet unable to break it off. Her love imprint had her attracted to men she couldn't trust and undermined her confidence to pick a suitable partner. "I can't trust love" was a double-edged sword that kept her losing trust in herself as well as the men she was attracted to.

To transform your hidden blocks to love, you must break the pattern of Your Love Imprint. The first step is to diagnose Your Love Imprint so you have the language of your core wound. This makes the unconscious hidden block tangible, so you know where to concentrate your efforts to heal your core wound, changing your results in love. This is the last step on your Awareness journey before moving on to the Transformation stage.

Love Imprint Examples

Your Love Imprint is the language of your core childhood wound. It's the code in your subconscious that highlights who you're attracted to and is the foundation of your struggles in love. Sharing these specific examples allows you to see how the underlying limiting belief system originates from your family of origin and then carries forward later in life to be played out in intimate relationships.

Michael—I will be disappointed by love

Michael is a single forty-three-year-old real estate agent who has limited experience dating. He's the middle child in an evangelical family who was initially rejected by his parents when he came out. Michael's family life appeared very stable; his parents have been married for over 50 years, and his siblings are both happily married. However, his mother was diagnosed with bipolar disorder, and he felt smothered by her and insecure about her emotional swings. His father traveled for work and was rarely at home.

Michael's dating life was driven by a fear that he wouldn't find his equal. He would play it safe and swing between dating stable older men or younger, passionate, creative men with no income. Due to his lack of self-esteem, he would never emotionally invest and was more of an observer than a participant in his romantic relationships. The belief that he would be disappointed by love turned into a self-fulfilling prophecy over and over again.

Souza—I am invisible in love

Souza is a single, never-married, forty-seven-year-old hospital technician from a close traditional family. As the oldest, she would help her mother around the house and took pride in being able to care for her siblings. Souza's strategies for earning love were shaped by focusing on other people's needs to the detriment of her own. From a young age she was attracted to girls, not boys like her friends, and this made her feel like an alien in her community. As a teenager, she tried to find someone like her in the community as she was desperate to alleviate her feelings of being different, but she did not succeed. Feeling like an alien caused Souza to jump into relationships quickly because the emotional and physical intimacy gave her the feeling of belonging that she never received in childhood. Rather than finding a beloved life partner, Souza ended up having many short-term relationships that left her feeling chronically heartbroken.

André—I'm not enough

André is a widowed fifty-nine-year-old human resources specialist. Raised in a military family with a strict father who was always disappointed by him and a mother focused on fitting in with the neighbors and supporting her husband's ambition, he never felt acknowledged or valued. His father died when he was sixteen years old, so he never had a chance to prove himself to his dad.

André is attracted to strong, powerful women, but he believes they are out of his league. He's had several relationships with women who want him to take care of them but doesn't find them satisfying. He's caught between feeling rejected and rejecting women he thinks are not worthy of him. Believing he is not enough, he ping-pongs between women he doesn't deserve and women he doesn't respect.

Rebecca—Love is for other people, not me

Rebecca is a single, never-married, Jewish fifty-one-year-old school teacher. She is the youngest of two children and was regularly and relentlessly teased by her older brother and father while growing up. She internalized their jesting to mean there is something inherently wrong with her and felt emotionally unsafe with the men in her family. Her mother was extremely conflict avoidant and wasn't capable of sticking up for her. Instead, she would downplay Rebecca's feelings and tell her to shrug it off.

Rebecca didn't have any romantic relationships until she was in college, initially dating men and later experimenting with women; she identified as lesbian for over a decade. In her late thirties, she started dating men again and found that the same issues followed her into those relationships. No relationships lasted more than a year, as she was very guarded and easily triggered. She had a long list of red flags to warn her and another list of qualities she desired in a partner. She was holding on tightly to the belief that love is for other people, but not for her.

* * *

Even these few examples show you the myriad ways that a childhood wound becomes the guiding force in who they find attractive and their struggles to find lasting love. When we diagnose a love imprint, it's the only time we take a comprehensive history and look at the patterns in their adult relationships and how those patterns mirror the dynamic from their family of origin. In this next exercise, you'll use all of the information you've gathered from the previous Love on Purpose Exercises to discover the language of Your Love Imprint. It's helpful to remember that Your Love Imprint is the language of a child, and it sums up the wounding story of your childhood. It's not an intellectual understanding of past events that you have as an adult. The words are your inner child's core wounding story, and the words will reflect that.

In Part II, you'll transform and heal Your Love Imprint so that it's no longer a driving force in your love life, allowing the adult version of you to select an ideal mate.

LOVE ON PURPOSE EXERCISE—THE LANGUAGE OF YOUR LOVE IMPRINT

Now it's your opportunity to diagnose your unique love imprint. You'll use all of your newfound awareness that you've discovered in the previous three chapters to bring clarity to your subconscious story of why lasting love has been difficult for you to create and sustain. The first step is to review your answers to the questions at the end of Chapter One.

1. Use the answers from the last exercise in Chapter One ("What patterns and repetitions do you notice?") to write down the patterns that repeat in your relationships. This pattern in your adult relationships is the first clue to the language of Your Love Imprint.

2. Look over your list of relationship fears in Question 1 (What are your biggest fears in relationship?) and narrow it down to a single overarching fear; for example, abandonment, being taken advantage of, making the wrong choice, not valued, growing old alone, rejected, and so on. Compare your biggest fear in relationship to your relationship history. How has this fear played out in your relationships?

3. Journal about your early childhood (ages 0–8) by answering the following questions: What was your parents' relationship like? How did they express love with each other? Were there issues with your siblings? Was anyone else involved in raising you (grandparent, step-parent, other extended family members, etc.)? Were there any traumatic events in your childhood, and how did they affect you?

4. Ask yourself these specific questions for each parent or care-giver: How did you know your Mom/Dad/caregiver loved you? How did they express their love for you? How would your Mom/Dad/caregiver respond when you were upset?

5. Using the following list as a guide, write down several sentences that express the essence of what you've discovered in the previous questions. They may be different ideas or variations on a theme. You're looking to sum it up in a simple sentence that pinpoints the wounding that you experienced. Your Love Imprint won't be a complicated intellectual explanation. It's the language of a child attempting to deal with their experience.

I'm not worthy of the love I want.

I'm unlovable.

Love is a mystery.

I have to earn love.

I'm unlucky in love.

Love is for other people, not me.

Love equals chaos.

I'm overlooked by love.

Love means I can't be satisfied.

Love is not safe.

I have to sacrifice for love.

I am invisible in love.

I don't count or matter in love.

I can't trust love.

I have to abandon myself for love.

I have to prove I'm lovable.

I don't deserve the love I want.

Love equals control.

My needs don't matter in love.

6. Looking at your list, read each statement one at a time to yourself. As you read each statement, drop your attention into your body and see how it lands with you. The right wording will elicit a visceral and/or emotional response in your body. It may feel like a punch to the gut, or your eyes may well up with tears, or you'll feel a powerful sadness or heaviness come over you. It's not an intellectual understanding. You'll feel it in your body when you get the correct language of your core wound.

Scan the QR code for bonus materials and video trainings:

PART 2

Transformation

5

The Four Keys to Self-Acceptance and Feeling Loved

"You, yourself, as much as anybody in the entire universe, deserve your love and affection."

—*Buddha*

The summer before meeting Orna, Matthew was in a relationship with Sarah, who on the surface appeared to be everything he was looking for in a life partner. They shared similar lifestyles and a vegan diet, both practiced yoga and meditation, and both had an interest in personal growth. She even had dark curly hair like the images he had put on his vision board in January of that year. Despite telling Matthew she liked him, she regularly found fault with him. She suggested a particular kind of workout regimen and criticized his chosen spiritual path. In many subtle and not-so-subtle ways she constantly told him he needed to change for her to accept him. Sarah's rejections and criticism could have put Matthew off, but instead he worked hard at making the changes she suggested. He thought he could win her affection and approval.

Sarah's criticisms echoed the teasing he experienced growing up with his older brothers and their friends. Her rejection matched his familiar internal experience, her judgment mirrored his self-judgment, and therefore she was a perfect match to Matthew's childhood wounds and love imprint. After a tumultuous three months together, he finally realized his attraction to Sarah was because of the rejection she kept dishing out. Like a lightning bolt striking him, the spell was broken, and that night he broke up with Sarah. Matthew told her, "I like myself. I like who I am, and I don't think I need to change to please anyone. I'm grateful for the opportunity you gave me to finally take a stand for myself."

Later that year, a few weeks into dating Orna, Matthew made an offhand self-deprecating comment. Immediately, she responded, "Be nice to this guy. You don't have to change a thing. Remember, you're perfect exactly as you are." For the first time, he was able to receive the compliment without hearing his inner voice arguing and judging himself. In that instant, Matthew could measure his growth and recognize that he finally accepted himself as is—warts and all. This was one of the earliest indications that Orna was different from all the other women he had dated. At last, Matthew finally transformed his pattern of seeking rejection (one of the strategies created by his love imprint) and let love in.

Transformation is the process of peeling away the layers of beliefs, habits, and strategies you developed to cope with your childhood emotional wounds, allowing you to become a more authentic version of yourself. You don't become a different person by changing these strategies; instead, you're allowing your authentic self to shine and be seen by the people in your life. Just as a lemon on a tree doesn't go from being solid green and hard to being soft ripe and yellow in an instant, transformation occurs gradually over a condensed period of time. Your transformation requires new actions consistently until the old way of being falls away and a new way of being emerges as a more confident, authentic, and happy version of yourself.

The first step on your journey of transformation is developing self-acceptance. Self-acceptance is having appreciation for all the parts of you—the good, the bad, and the ugly. It's through self-acceptance that you learn to love yourself and open your heart to let love in from another person. Self-acceptance comes before any of the other steps of transformation because you can't change the parts of you that you're judging. Renowned Swiss psychologist Carl Jung taught, "What you resist persists." Judgment of *what is* keeps you stuck in the problem. It's only by accepting who you are and how you got here that you can create the changes you desire.

The journey of self-acceptance is a process of letting go of the resistance to who you've been to create space for who you're becoming. This is not passive acceptance. Make a fist with your right hand then push it into the palm of your left hand while resisting. These two energies pushing against each other is the internal experience of self-criticism and judgment. Now, stop resisting with your left hand and continue pushing with your right. You'll discover the energy moves and then dissipates because there's no longer any resistance to it. This is how acceptance releases your internal struggle and frees you to create change.

> *The journey of self-acceptance is a process of letting go of the resistance to who you've been to create space for who you're becoming.*

The four keys to self-acceptance provide a map to adjust your strategies and behaviors and to develop compassion for your shortcomings, mistakes, and faults. By embracing these four concepts and applying them to your life, you'll gradually come to accept yourself as you are without judgment. When judgment is one of the strategies created by Your Love Imprint, it's the biggest block to love; nothing else even comes close. It leaves you feeling unworthy of the love you desire. If you're in a habit of judging yourself, you'll never measure up to your unrealistic expectations of self, and no person will ever measure up to your unrealistic expectations.

Judgment is the opposite of love and acceptance. Everyone desires to be loved unconditionally, and yet most people are unable to love themselves unequivocally. In an intimate relationship, water seeks its own level, meaning your partner will energetically match your ability to accept yourself. As you come to terms with loving yourself as imperfect as you are, you'll live a much happier life and be able to accept the shortcomings of your life partner too.

The First Key to Self-Acceptance—You Are Not Your Behaviors

It's easy to mistake your identity with your behaviors, but they aren't the same thing. Behaviors are a collection of habits and strategies that you've learned over the years. Some behaviors are hereditary (through genetic transmission), some are learned through cultural transmission (parenting and childhood environment), and others you've created on your own. Your identity, who you are, is not a collection of your thoughts and behaviors. If you were to change your thoughts and behaviors, you wouldn't become a different person—your identity doesn't change.

Your emotional state can also be conflated with your identity by saying things like, "I'm depressed," or "I'm angry." The correct speech is, "I feel . . ." not "I am . . . ," because your feelings are a temporary sensation that you're experiencing, not a permanent condition of your identity. The depression will pass, as well as the anger; they're not fixtures of your character. If you believe you're emotionally unavailable, or you're codependent, or you're too needy, then those beliefs become part of how you view yourself rather than as strategies you learned to deal with stressful situations. You perceive them as facts rather than temporary behaviors because you tie them to your character. It's nearly impossible to change these unwelcome behaviors if you decide they are an integral part of your identity.

You may ask yourself, "Who am I without my thoughts, feelings, and behaviors?" We believe that every person is born as the physical embodiment of the energy of love. You're here to express love, to receive love, to be love; that's the truth of who you are. In essence, you are love. Every religion and spiritual tradition embodies a version of this universal truth. You don't have to believe in any kind of religion or spirituality to know that you have a moral obligation to treat other human beings with kindness and compassion. The challenge is to see past your behavior to see the child within, who learned that love was conditional in your family of origin, and only developed the beliefs and strategies of Your Love Imprint to feel loved and safe in the world. Those beliefs are not who you are; they're adjustments you made to the conditions of your upbringing. Accepting this truth allows you to accept *your inherent lovability.* Every person is "perfectly imperfect," and you are no exception. You came into the world like every other human baby. You accepted love from anyone willing to give it, and you shined the spotlight of love on anyone present. It's why being around a baby is so joyful—they have no blocks to love.

> *Every person is born as the physical embodiment of the energy of love.*

Jacqui found it extremely difficult to admit she was a good person. In her childhood she struggled with her weight, was bullied, and didn't fit in. Her love imprint, "Love is for other people, not me," created the self-limiting belief that she was not a good person. Her younger brother had behavioral issues and took up all the emotional oxygen in the family. The anxiety she felt about her brother's outbursts and her fear of letting her mother down developed into a habit of procrastination. She was working in an industry with hard deadlines, yet she worked independently, so she managed her entire schedule. The constant challenge to meet her deadlines led her to believe there was something inherently wrong with her. In her mind, the procrastination for dealing with stress had become part of Jacqui's identity. She never missed a deadline; however, she would sacrifice sleep, eat poorly, and neglect her basic self-care in order to meet a deadline.

Finally, Jacqui accepted that procrastination was a behavior she learned as a child to navigate her difficult family dynamic rather than a flaw in her character. As her internal dialog softened, she stopped relentlessly judging herself, something that had carried over into her dating life. She had a tendency to become emotionally attached the moment she felt an instant attraction, especially if the guy she liked gave her mixed messages. Jacqui's procrastination strategy was part of a shame cycle, where her procrastination caused her to feel bad about herself and therefore caused her to procrastinate even more. Her dating habits fit this same pattern, choosing quickly without evaluating whether or not the guy had the capacity to meet her needs and be a good partner for her, and then feeling bad about herself when he inevitably disappointed her. She learned to slow down the dating process and delay exclusivity. She became an observer and more relaxed, which allowed her to evaluate her dates over time. Rather than accepting the crumbs a guy was willing to give her, she started cutting loose the ones who were unreliable, hot/cold, and flaky. She's no longer experiencing dating burnout because she's off the rollercoaster of hope and disappointment. Jacqui's behaviors and mindset are now aligned with being worthy of love. It's just a matter of time until she meets an ideal match, and her mindset is on track for lasting love.

The Second Key to Self-Acceptance—All Your Behavior Has Positive Intent

It's common to judge yourself for self-sabotaging behaviors. However, when you realize that these behaviors aren't intended to impede your progress or hurt you, then you can let go of self-judgment. No matter the result, these behaviors are actually trying to get you something you need. Every action you take is attempting to fulfill a need, for example love, safety, approval, or acceptance; however, not all your behavior garners a positive result. The majority of your behavior is habitual, and your habits were originally meant to help you survive (even if they get in the way of your ability to thrive). When you accept that a behavior (even a self-sabotaging one) isn't trying to harm you, instead it's trying to help you, then you can stop judging the behavior, which opens space for compassion and acceptance.

This adjustment in your perspective of self creates an opportunity to learn a new behavior, one that's more effective at getting your needs met. For example, say you had a painful experience in a relationship because you overlooked a red flag, so you vowed to never let that happen to you again. Maybe you became hyper-aware of possible red flags to protect yourself from heartbreak and feeling duped. You became preoccupied with finding red flags due to one specific painful experience and applied this preoccupation to every possible match. So you reject all potential dates because at one time someone hurt you. Your brain designed this strategy to keep you safe from being hurt again, which shows the positive intent, but the result is actually not productive because it will be difficult to find anyone who transcends your criticism. This is like getting food poisoning at a restaurant and deciding to never eat out again. However, accepting that your strategy of looking for red flags was developed as a way to keep you safe empowers you to let go of your judgment of the behavior and create a bet-

The understanding that all your behavior has positive intent allows you to release self-judgment and simply look for new strategies with better results.

ter strategy, one that doesn't have you rejecting all potential partners. The understanding that all your behavior has positive intent allows you to release self-judgment and simply look for new strategies with better results. Releasing that self-judgment allows you to feel grateful for your bad strategies and all the effort they've put in to try to help you. Imagine these behaviors are like a good friend with bad advice. That doesn't make them a bad friend or mean they don't care about you; you simply know not to take their guidance or counsel.

In order to develop a nonjudgmental mindset, evaluate your behavior based on the results you get instead of judging yourself for having the bad habit in the first place. Using our previous example of ignoring red flags, imagine a new strategy of waiting until you're certain a person you're attracted to is well-intentioned, with similar life goals and shared values. Because of your past experiences, you can utilize discernment and remain curious rather than immediately deselecting them for trivial reasons. When you're not giving a stranger the benefit of the doubt until they've earned it, you're able to keep your heart open to the possibility of love, as well as keep yourself safe from partners that aren't a good match for you.

Gabriella was raised by a single mom. Her father had left them soon after she was born and was never part of her upbringing. Gabriella and her mother were very close; it was always the two of them against the world. Filled with hurt and anger, her mother was particularly critical of Gabriella's father and had nothing good to say about men in general. While Gabriella didn't have any negative experiences with men cheating, lying, or otherwise being deceitful, she had a deep-seated distrust of men. It was as if she'd made a contract with her mother when she was a little girl to be skeptical of all men (even now after her mother had long passed away).

Gabriella's strategy of distrusting men stemmed from wanting to feel loved—a positive intent, yet her behavior garnered the opposite result. She never consciously decided to keep herself lonely and single until well into her fifties, and yet her natural desire to feel loved by her mother required her to buy into her mother's prejudice. By making her unconscious strategy conscious, Gabriella was able to break the pact with her mother. Not long after, she met a great man, and they've created a fulfilling and lasting relationship.

The Third Key to Self-Acceptance—All Judgment Is Self-Judgment

The qualities that you judge in someone else reflect a wound or judgment you have about yourself. For example, if you're afraid of making a mistake and don't want to disappoint your partner, it's easy to interpret their curiosity and questions as an attack and get defensive. Or if you're a perfectionist who's highly critical of yourself, it's easy to get angry at your partner when they mess up. Judgment in intimate relationships is like a funhouse mirror: The image in the mirror is distorted so you don't realize that it's you in the reflection.

The realization that all judgment is self-judgment changes your perspective so you can take responsibility for your own fears, criticisms, and frustrations. This shift in focus puts you in the driver's seat to create change simply by being able to feel compassion for your shortcomings. Compassion is the antidote to judgment. If you saw someone in a hurry frantically running down a crowded street, your mind may judge them for being reckless, nearly crashing into people. If you found out their child was in the hospital and they were rushing to get there, your judgment would melt away with compassion for their situation.

Releasing judgment will make all your relationships better, especially the one you have with yourself.

Train your mind to release judgment by accessing compassion. It might be easier for you to start with others and then work on compassion for self, or maybe you more readily can find compassion for yourself first and then others. Try it out both ways and discover the one that's more amenable for you. Releasing judgment will make all your relationships better, especially the one you have with yourself.

Isabella was the caretaker in her family, and even as a little girl she was the peacekeeper, always working to see that everyone got along. As the oldest child and the only girl, she internalized her father's distaste for emotions and learned to swallow her own. She even put her life on hold to care for them as octogenarians. Expressing her needs and wants was completely foreign to her (her love imprint is "I am rejected by love") and as we learned about her experiences with love and dating, we noticed something interesting: She always found fault with the men who were available for a relationship and would end it. However, she found it easy to invest her heart in men who were emotionally distant or lived far away. She would cling to these unavailable men as if they were her last hope. Isabella's judgment of emotionally available men was the funhouse mirror reflection of herself, the projection of her own inadequacies. Her focus on nurturing others to her own detriment had left her feeling needy and unworthy, so she unconsciously pushed away opportunities for love by seeing available men as unworthy too. Isabella's feelings of worthlessness would not allow her to accept an available partner. She told us she didn't find the men that pursued her attractive, but what was really at play was her own self-judgment.

The first step in Isabella's journey to lasting love was to identify her feeling state (rather than being absorbed with her thoughts) and then determine her terms for love. Her progress allowed her to become comfortable with expressing her feelings and making requests instead of judging herself for having feelings and needs. Isabella's entire dating process shifted to identify an ideal partner who had the capacity to meet her needs rather than being run through the lens of her self-judgement. She's still looking for her ideal match, but she's no longer pushing away men who are emotionally available and pursuing her for a relationship. The fun part for Isabella is that she's enjoying the dating process and finds that she has more requests for dates than she has time for (a complete one-eighty from the days when she struggled to find anyone to date).

The Fourth Key to Self-Acceptance—The Love You Seek Is Inside of You

You don't get love from another person; you share love with them. It's the love you have for yourself that is reflected back to you

It's the love you have for yourself that is reflected back to you through the eyes of your beloved.

through the eyes of your beloved. Loving and accepting yourself allows you to receive love from another person. It allows you to break the pattern of seeking a love imprint match because your mind is no longer highlighting the familiar dynamic from childhood. The importance of loving and accepting yourself is that you'll have a hard time trusting that someone else will love and accept you if you don't. It feels weird, like when Matthew was chasing rejection, the women who were interested in him were all a turn off.

In his twenties, Matthew didn't like himself very much. When he met a woman who was interested in him, his first thought would be, "What's wrong with her?" Followed by, "Wait until she gets to know me; she'll see what's wrong with me." These beliefs along with his inner critic motivated his self-sabotaging behavior. It was only after Matthew's commitment to self-acceptance that he was able to receive Orna's love. He'd finally broken his pattern of self-sabotage.

The risk of loving another person becomes moot when you realize that you cannot lose love because love comes from within. Searching for someone to fill the holes inside of you, to complete you, will lead you down a path of dysfunctional, codependent, unhealthy, and unsustainable relationships. Your beloved won't complete you; they'll understand you. They'll love you for your flaws, not despite them. If someone showed up loving and accepting you before you loved and accepted yourself, on some level you would reject them. You'd feel unworthy, or it would feel odd to spend time with them because you'd be suspicious of them. Self-acceptance is the first step in learning to love yourself. Aim for self-acceptance, and self-love will automatically follow.

Tanisha was raised in a chaotic environment by a narcissistic mother who treated her like an afterthought. She worked hard to get her mother's attention and would do anything to win her love and approval. Sadly she was always met with criticism or indifference. Tanisha internalized her mother's behavior, creating the core wound of her love imprint as a belief that she didn't count or matter. She spent most of her adulthood pining for emotionally unavailable or married men. Because she didn't value herself, she tried to be useful to each of her partners in an effort to ingratiate herself to him so he wouldn't leave her. Inevitably the breakup came, proving once again that she could never be good enough for any man to stay.

A big part of our journey with Tanisha was teaching her to love and accept herself, even the parts she didn't like very much, and to break her pattern of trying to earn love. Having spent years in personal growth seminars, she would immediately offer suggestions on improving the lives of the guys she was dating. At one point we called her out on coaching a potential boyfriend; it was just another strategy for being useful to him. To drive the point home, we asked, "Do you want to be his mother or his lover?" She insisted that coaching these guys was part of her personality, and that she was simply being "authentic." This pushed us to come up with our clear definition of authenticity: to identify your feelings and share them with another person. (This is also meant to give you an action to take, rather than the vague and elusive "Just be yourself" through the dating process.)

When another guy she got hooked on disappeared, rather than riding the familiar rollercoaster of despair to hope, she embraced being on her own for a while. This was the first pause she'd ever taken to spend quality time with herself. She quit a job with an abusive boss and found a better one with a much higher salary, better benefits, and an employer that valued her. She took up new hobbies, made some new friends, and when she started dating again she was able to break her lifelong habit of seeking validation. After a few months, she met Johnny, and it didn't start with her old familiar head-over-heels, all-consuming, obsessive thinking—it was a completely new experience. She'd almost passed on meeting him the first time and wasn't sure about him for a few dates. He was consistent, thoughtful, and his actions matched his words. He embraces all of Tanisha's quirky personality traits and expresses his love for her every single day. She says that falling for Johnny snuck up on her.

Perfectionism and Self-Acceptance

Abigail grew up in a home ruled by her father as if he was a king. The entire family bent to his moods, his criticisms, and his emotional abuse. He kept everyone on their toes, particularly Abigail. As the oldest, she had the highest expectations placed on her, and she also became the family peacekeeper, sacrificing her wants and needs to take care of her three younger siblings. She always put everyone in her family first, addressing their needs, their desires, and their goals. After her mother passed away, she reached out to us because she knew she didn't want to spend the rest of her life alone. The real problem was that she couldn't ever allow herself to make a mistake.

We first caught on to Abigail's unrealistic expectations for herself when she spoke with us about a group of female friends; there was one particular woman that Abigail struggled to connect with. She always felt like she had done something wrong and would spin in her mind for days ruminating on every uncomfortable interaction. Abigail believed that if she could just find the right words, or not take her friend's behavior so personally, she could bridge the gap between them and find a way to connect. Unfortunately, there was nothing Abigail could do to change the dynamic between them, because Abigail wasn't the problem. She finally stopped trying to twist into a pretzel and do everything right for this friend and started expressing herself authentically. Quickly Abigail discovered this woman wasn't emotionally available for a deeper connection and that she wasn't a very good friend after all. This was the first time in Abigail's life that she gave up on someone—in her sixties! Letting go of her peacekeeper strategies and releasing her perfectionism was the beginning of her transformation.

Acknowledging and accepting all her wonderful qualities allowed Abigail to be okay with some of her characteristics she disliked. Finally realizing that she had to accept her own faults in order to partner with another imperfect person was a gamechanger for her love life. The man she's married to now loves and accepts her as is, even when she feels disappointed or makes requests. He tells her all the time he wants to be her hero and make her happier.

Perfectionism is detrimental to your love life because it goes hand in hand with an active inner critic and unrealistic expectations. If everything has to be perfect it will be nearly impossible for any human to meet your expectations. Plus, you'd be constantly disappointing yourself, which makes it hard for you to believe that someone else will love you. Ultimately, having integrity doesn't mean you never make a mistake; having integrity is how you behave when you make one. Whatever the root of your perfectionism—fear of failure, unworthiness, or needing to prove you're lovable—there will be negative consequences in your love life. Allowing yourself to make mistakes and feeling compassion for yourself when you do, opens the possibility for you to receive love. Letting go of how you think things are supposed to be frees you to be more loving and compassionate with yourself and a potential partner. You are not required to be perfect to have great love in your life. Loving yourself exactly as you are creates opportunities to let love in.

> *Having integrity doesn't mean you never make a mistake; having integrity is how you behave when you make one.*

In the 1990s, Orna's friend taught her how to knit, and when she proudly displayed the nearly completed scarf she'd been working on he told her to make another row, goof up the pattern, and then he'd show her how to finish the scarf by casting off (securing all the stitches so they don't unravel). After spending so much time making sure the stitches were all correct, Orna was confused and asked with hesitation, "You mean make a mistake *on purpose?*" Her friend replied, "Yes, only machines are perfect. The mistake is the mark that the scarf was made by human hands." As a perfectionist this landed strongly with Orna, who had been reassessing her inner dialog at the time. She already knew she was very hard on herself, but what her friend just shared about knitting can be applied to other things in life as well. Trying to be "perfect" had consumed much of Orna's life and had created a lot of unhappiness. Accepting that humans make mistakes, she released the unrealistic expectation of being perfect and decided she would always do her best instead.

Learning to let her best be good enough was revolutionary for Orna. The affirmation, "I am perfectly imperfect," was born out of this experience. As Orna moved through her life with this newfound self-acceptance and compassion she was able to interact with people on a higher level. She found that critical people were unhappy, and those who were happy weren't obsessed with being perfect. Her new goal was to be kind and loving to herself no matter what, so when she made a mistake she'd say, "Well, it sure sucks not being perfect!" And then she would work on a solution for the issue at hand. Every team member at Creating Love on Purpose knows this phrase because making a mistake is human and being perfect is not a realistic expectation. When you can accept yourself along with all your faults and shortcomings, you'll find that you're happier and more open to receive love. One day soon you'll be sharing your life with your beloved, and when they make a mistake you can tell them, "You're perfectly imperfect and your best is good enough."

Accept yourself along with all your faults and shortcomings, you'll find that you're happier and more open to receive love.

LOVE ON PURPOSE EXERCISES

Self-acceptance lays the groundwork for you to transform your mental/emotional patterns that no longer serve you. You must first accept yourself as is, and then you're ready to change the habits and strategies that no longer serve you.

The following exercises are pattern interrupts intended to break your habitual negative and judgmental thoughts. These tools are useful in interrupting the pattern of an emotional story that isn't serving you, allowing you to quickly transition to a more resourceful state. Shift your mindset by releasing self-criticism and judgment, and you'll open a path to self-love and acceptance and ultimately paving the way to your beloved.

Laughter Exercise

This simple but effective exercise is a perfect tool for rewiring your mental/emotional relationship to negative events in your life. When you retell the details of a hurtful or frustrating experience while laughing out loud, you rewire your emotional response to the event. Laughter releases dopamine, oxytocin, serotonin, and endorphins, even when you fake it. Laughing while recounting a painful experience will have the effect of transforming your emotional response to the event.

It might be difficult to imagine yourself laughing about something serious or traumatic; however, fake laughing will give you all the benefits of real laughter, so get ready to fake it until you make it!

Three sounds make up laughter: Ho, Ha, and He. Vocalizing each sound three at a time gives you an easy way to start. Place your hands on your lower belly, take a deep breath into your navel, and then begin to fake laugh: "Ho! Ho! Ho!" "Ha! Ha! Ha!" "He! He! He!" Very quickly you'll actually be laughing. Laughter is infectious and contagious. Once you have a good laugh going, tell the story of the upsetting event out loud while laughing hysterically.

Just like learning to do anything new, this may take some getting used to, and practice makes perfect. Asking a friend to help, or doing this exercise with a group taking turns sharing stories makes this exercise easier and much more fun.

Bracelet Exercise

Remember those negative thought patterns you identified in Chapter Three? This exercise interrupts the pattern and creates a new positive thought habit to replace them. Becoming aware of your inner dialog brings your unconscious habit into your conscious awareness. Now you have a choice about the habit and can begin the process of changing it.

Find yourself a stretchy bracelet. It can be a silicone wristband, a beaded bracelet, a rubber band, or a hair tie. The key is that it's easy to slide off and slide back on. First thing in the morning place the bracelet on your right wrist, so you have a consistent starting point. Choose one of the negative thought patterns or beliefs you've identified that triggers you to feel bad about yourself, or your relationship prospects, that you'd like to change.

During the day when you notice the negative thought, take the bracelet off your wrist as you say to yourself, "Cancel, cancel, cancel!" (while shaking your head no). Replace the thought with an affirmation that either contradicts that belief or affirms your positive qualities as you place the bracelet on your left wrist. For example, you could change "I never get what I want" to "My desires come to me easily and effortlessly." Change "I'm too old for love" to "Love is my birthright!" Or change "Love isn't meant to be for me" to "Love is for everyone, especially me!"

Throughout the day, keep paying attention to your inner dialog, interrupting the negative thought pattern that you want to change and replacing the negative thought with a positive one, all while moving the bracelet back and forth. Make this a daily practice and see if you can go an hour without moving the bracelet, then a whole day, then a week, and set a goal of 40 days without moving the bracelet. Then move on to another negative thought pattern and start transforming it. View the following chart for inspiration to turn negative thoughts into positive ones, and feel free to come up with your own.

Negative Thought	**New Positive Thought**
"No one will ever love me."	"I am loveable exactly as I am."
"I never get what I want."	"My desires come to me easily and effortlessly."
"How come _____ has it so easy when it's so hard for me?"	"I'm open to receive all my good. My journey is unique."
"It's so hard to meet people."	"I meet new people wherever I go."
"I'm too old for love."	"Love is my birthright!"
"Online dating sucks."	"Dating lets me practice discernment."
"I'm too picky."	"My match will love me as is."
"I'll have to give up my freedom."	"Freedom comes from commitment to the right person."
"No one understands me."	"I am complex and I love that about me."
"Love isn't meant to be for me."	"Love is for everyone especially me!"
"I always screw things up."	"I'm okay making mistakes that's how I learn to do better."

Scan the QR code for bonus materials and video trainings:

6

Mastering Your Emotional Life

"The secret of change is to focus all your energy, not on fighting the old, but on building the new."

—Dan Millman

Breaking the relationship patterns in Your Love Imprint requires you to change your relationship with your emotional life and embrace being authentic. You'll no longer be able to keep your feelings to yourself because you're afraid of conflict or that you'll be rejected. The only way to create emotional connection is to share your feelings, even when it's uncomfortable. Minimizing your expectations and desires because you don't believe you

An emotionally intimate relationship allows you to feel understood, to relax, and be yourself.

deserve more or you're imagining negative outcomes are strategies that prevent you from creating a healthy relationship. An emotionally intimate relationship allows you to feel understood, to relax, and be yourself—to be loved and accepted as you are without having to become an emotional shapeshifter trying to earn love, approval, or acceptance.

There's an important distinction between honesty and authenticity. Honesty is important in all your relationships; however, people can use honesty as an excuse to communicate their judgments and opinions of you and your behavior. You've likely had the experience of someone pulling you aside by asking, "Can I be honest with you?" And what you get is a large dose of their opinion of you. This is not authentic, because how someone feels about you is not a fact; it's subjective. When you share how you feel by simply expressing your emotional state, you're taking full responsibility for it.

Authenticity isn't about expressing your opinion; it's about expressing your truth. Authenticity has become a bit of a buzz-word, and its overuse has diluted its meaning. In your quest for long-lasting love, the only useful definition of "being authentic" is *to identify your feelings and share them with another person*. This isn't to say your emotions are the most important thing, because as we discussed earlier, your feelings are temporary, and they're constantly changing. The act of being authentic is identifying your emotional state in the present moment and sharing it—not the meaning you've assigned to your emotions, your opinions, or your emotional stories. Identifying and expressing your feelings is the only way to create emotional connection with another person. Even if you don't get the response you'd hoped for, you'll still feel better by acknowledging your feelings. It's like sending a message to the Universe that you count, and you matter.

The key to being authentic is to identify your emotional experience regardless of other people's thoughts or feelings. Imagine you're at a figurative emotional restaurant. Many people sit at the table and wait to see what everyone else is ordering before placing their order. How you feel has nothing to do with how all the other people at the table feel. Jockeying your position based on other people's feelings is *inauthentic*. Sitting at the table and expressing yourself without worrying about, or comparing yourself to everyone else, is being authentic.

If you come from a family where expressing negative emotions was forbidden or frowned upon, this may be extra difficult for you. Remember, the only way to create emotional connection with another person is to be authentic and speak your truth. You'll find the people in your life who truly care about you want to know your feelings, and they'll even be willing to make adjustments so you feel better when you spend time with them. These caring people aren't mind readers; you'll have to speak up to discover if they're capable of acknowledging your feelings. You have the opportunity to create a new level of connection with them as you transform your communication style.

The biggest mistake people make is to judge the success of their communication by the response they get from the other person. This puts all the power in the hands of the other person without taking their triggers, wounds, or capacity into account. The only way to judge the success of your communication is by one measure: How authentic you're able to be. Upon sharing this with our client Barbara, she exclaimed,

The only way to judge the success of your communication is by one measure: How authentic you're able to be.

"That's amazing, because that takes manipulation out of the equation altogether!" Being authentic allows you to evaluate the capacity of the other person based on their response. You're able to evaluate who they are and what they're capable of in the moment. Being authentic allows you to own your feelings one hundred percent, so you don't have to downplay something that's very upsetting, and if you're triggered, you can catch yourself making a mountain out of a molehill.

Years ago, Orna had a boyfriend who told her during a disagreement she was overreacting. Her response was, "Where's the meter?" When she saw his perplexed face, she continued, "Where's the meter that shows I'm in the red? I'm reacting in a way that you don't like, but I'm not *over* anything, I'm very upset and this is appropriate for how I feel in this moment."

The Steps to Emotional Authenticity

To master your emotional life and create connection in your relationships, you'll need new tools to identify your feelings and express them in a productive way so you can be heard. The Steps to Emotional Authenticity are your marathon training for working out at the "authenticity gym." You go to the gym to build strength and stamina through resistance. The authenticity gym builds your authenticity muscles by helping you push through your own resistance to share your emotional truth. People who decide to run a marathon don't go out and run twenty-six miles; they start off by trying to run one mile, and then add on. You'll take the same approach to build your authenticity muscles.

To begin, look over the following steps and determine where you tend to get tripped up or stuck. Practice and become adept at that step before attempting to implement the next one. Don't try to master all five of these steps at once; just put effort toward practicing them by adding on one at a time, like adding miles to train for a marathon. Let go of any expectation of perfection. We teach this every day of the week, and we still mess this up sometimes. Your effort counts, and with people in your life you'll have the opportunity to clean up misunderstandings if your interaction gets messy. You're going to have to let your best efforts be good enough as you practice this lifelong skill of speaking up for yourself and sharing your truth. The benefits are extraordinary, and your relationship with yourself will significantly improve.

*   *   *

The Steps to Emotional Authenticity are as follows:

1. Identify emotion
2. Express it
3. With the person you're having it with
4. In the moment that it's happening
5. At the appropriate intensity

Step One (Identify emotion) is a one-word emotion that you can plug into this sentence: "I feel _____[fill in the blank]_____."

If you tend to confuse your thoughts and your feelings (and most people do), here's a quick way to know the difference: If you say, "I think we should go to the store and get some milk," that's a thought, because it makes logical sense. If you say, "I think _____[fill in the blank]_____," and it doesn't make sense, or it sounds like caveman talk, then you've plugged in an emotion—which doesn't make logical sense. For example, "I think angry," or "I think bliss." Emotions aren't linear or logical; however, all your emotions are body sensations (going back to Chapter Two). Don't smoosh your thoughts and feelings together by making it grammatically correct with, "I think I feel _____[fill in the blank]_____." Separating your thoughts from your feelings in this way will help make your workout at the authenticity gym more productive. These steps compound, so as you succeed with steps one and two, you'll add on the next step, and then the next, one at a time.

Step Two (Express it) means to express your feelings out loud to yourself or to a third party (not yet with the person who sparked the emotion). For example, you're expressing your feelings to a friend about your date, but not yet with the person you're dating. Speaking your feelings allows you to acknowledge them. Recognizing your feeling state is basic self-care, and your feelings are always appropriate, but the actions you may take due to your feelings are not always appropriate. As mentioned earlier, feeling irate about someone's behavior is appropriate. If you kill them because you feel irate, that's not appropriate.

Step Three (With the person you're having it with) is to express your feelings with the applicable person, but at this point in your training you're only expressing your feeling state after the fact (not in the moment). Please don't go looking for disagreements months or years ago and bring them up. It's much better when it's a recent event, fresh in your mind (and the other person's mind too). There will always be plenty of opportunities to speak up with the people in your life. Rather than looking backward, aim to share your truth from here on out as best you can, particularly when you've become upset and can recognize and identify your emotional state after the fact.

Step Four (In the moment that it's happening) is where most people get tripped up because generally those who do speak up often like to wait and script it out or think about how to say it rather than broaching the subject as it's occurring. This will feel uncomfortable, and it may always feel a little scary. Start by practicing with the people in your inner circle first, the ones who care about you and are most able to give you some leeway.

Don't worry about your level of intensity yet; that's like the professional marathon runner who's trying to win the race. Instead, be like most people running a marathon; they're aiming for a personal best. The only person you're competing with is yourself and your efforts.

Step Five (At the appropriate intensity) requires finesse, because your intensity of emotion can depend on a couple of things. If a person exhibited a particular behavior that you don't care for, and you bottled up your feelings for too long so you flew off the handle, that's not appropriate because it was your choice not to have spoken up sooner. You're responsible for bottling up that emotion until you burst, not the other person. With your intensity of expression, also consider that all your emotions compound. Your upset in the moment is influenced by your emotional stories. The person you're interacting with is not responsible for all the times you've felt a particular emotion or that you're now triggered. (You'll discover how to address being triggered in the skills for lasting love in Part III.) Practice tempering your expression if you've not spoken up about it earlier, and take responsibility for not doing so. This last step is like a cherry on top of an ice cream sundae. You've got this!

The Steps to Emotional Authenticity are for you, so you can track yourself and work through the five steps, growing from one to the next rather than trying to master all five steps at once. Chunking it down to just grow to the next step is essential for success. Now, let's cover how you implement these steps along with leveraging your communication so the other person can hear you. To implement your newfound authentic voice, you'll practice and embrace the Speak How You Feel Template.

The Walters' SHYFT Communication Blueprint

Effective emotional communication isn't taught in schools, nor do most people have good role models showing them how to speak up and share their feelings. It becomes even more stress-inducing if they need to make a request. In the 1970s, clinical psychologist Marshall Rosenberg developed Non-Violent Communication as a way to increase empathy and understanding by taking responsibility for your emotions and making a request to get your needs met. We've taken these ideas and put them into a succinct communication template that gives you a tool for communicating your emotional authenticity. It's just as effective for communicating positive feelings as it is for communicating negative feelings, and it contains three important components to creating connection and working through disagreements.

The first component is to identify how you feel and express it (steps one and two from the Steps to Emotional Authenticity) beginning with an "I feel" statement. The second component is to put your feelings into context. They don't exist in a vacuum, and giving them context allows you to discuss the situation without placing blame or responsibility on the other person. The final component is to offer a resolution or solution by making a request. You can talk about anything when you have the communication tools to express your feeling state with the Speak How You Feel Template (SHYFT).

If you want to show up authentically, you must use this SHYFT:

"I feel _____[one-word emotion]_____, when ____[context]____."

You can stop here and simply practice speaking your truth. It's better if you can offer a joint solution or make a direct request. Here are those options:

A. "Can we please ____[joint solution]____.

Or

B. "Would you please ____[direct request]____.

Here's an example of using the SHYFT: "I feel **neglected** (one word emotion) when **the garbage isn't taken out** (context). Would you please **make an effort to notice when the garbage is full and take it out as needed** (direct request)?" We often use this example because it brings up our society's obsession with analysis. People question the validity of their feelings because they wonder *why* they feel neglected if the garbage isn't taken out. Knowing *why* isn't as important as understanding that your feelings are valid and you have a right to feel how you do. Also, focusing on why you feel the way you do won't change your emotional state and can have you trying to justify your feelings. Your feelings are valid whether you know *why* you feel neglected or not. Your goal is to acknowledge and express your emotions because when you do **your feelings will shift and change.** You'll feel better having spoken your truth, and you'll have given the other person an opportunity to know you and see you.

Write down and memorize the SHYFT. We encourage you to embrace this template and practice it at every opportunity in your personal life. When you're authentic and speak your truth, it's as if you've sent the other person an invitation to join you at an authenticity party. Just like an actual party, some people will be available to attend, and others won't. Don't assume you know who has the capacity to join you and be authentic and who doesn't—people can always surprise you. This blueprint is tried and true. It's not improved by starting with "when"; be sure you always begin with "I." Commit the SHYFT to memory and practice it until it becomes natural for you to express your feelings this way.

Another way to use this template is to make a request by letting someone know how you *would* feel if they took a particular action. When we started dating, Matthew wasn't the kind of man who opened a woman's car door. One evening at Orna's apartment, she said to him, "I feel cherished when a man opens the car door. Would you please open the car door for me when we go out?" Matthew said, "Oh, you like that? Sure, yeah I can do that!" It took some time for Matthew to make opening the car door a new habit, and Orna was always kind and patient when he forgot. All these years later, Matthew still opens Orna's car door. Once, back in Matthew's hometown with family, he tried to open the car door for his sister-in-law, and she started yelling at him, "I can get my own damn door!" Both of us had to refrain from laughing; it was quite comical.

Don't make assumptions about why someone does or doesn't do something; instead, just let them know your preferences. The right match for you will want to know how to please you and make you happy. Expressing yourself will always give you the information you're looking for. Practice the SHYFT without the unrealistic expectation that you'll be perfect at it. Remember, even doctors are just *practicing* medicine. Practice being authentic, and you'll find that all your relationships benefit. Release any judgment about your ability to execute the SHYFT and instead let your best efforts be good enough.

Make every effort to eliminate the word "you" when putting your feelings into context. It's more effective to say, "I feel neglected when the garbage isn't taken out" than to say, "I feel neglected when *you* don't take out the garbage." For one thing, your feelings aren't about the other person; they're connected to the circumstances. If someone else wasn't taking out the garbage, you'd still feel neglected. The other very important part of memorizing this template, practicing it, and utilizing it as often as possible is that it leverages the opportunity for you to be heard by the other person. By starting with "I feel . . ." you're taking responsibility for your feelings and not pointing the finger at the other person or accusing them of anything.

It's very important to note that this is *not* a magical template that gets people to behave the way you want them to. (If you find that magic template, please let us know.) There's no way for you to control other people and get them to behave in a certain way. In life, you only have control over *your* thoughts, feelings, and actions. Using this template reveals who's capable of making an adjustment and who's unwilling or unable to. Are they able to hear you? Can they meet you at the high vibration of authenticity and share their feelings? Do they argue with you or try to discount your emotions? Do they make you bad or wrong for your feeling state?

When you work out at the authenticity gym, you become stronger by pushing through your fear of how the other person may respond. It's appropriate to feel discomfort when you risk by expressing your truth, but you'll find the rewards are great. It may always feel scary for you; however, when you're able to be authentic and the other person can share their authentic self, you've created the opportunity for emotional intimacy.

We urge you to take your time and be kind to yourself as you get the hang of this new way of communicating. There's a natural learning curve that you go through as you acquire a new skill. Being mindful of this learning curve will give you the patience and compassion you need to master authentic communication.

Years ago, we were visiting Matthew's family and spent the afternoon bowling with his brother, sister-in-law, and their kids. Our eight-year-old nephew had never been bowling before and was very hard on himself that he was losing. He expected to somehow be an expert at bowling his first time at the lanes. Playing against grown-ups (even those who didn't go bowling very often), this young lad was having a tough time. At one point in the afternoon, he had a full-fledged meltdown. Talk about an unrealistic expectation!

It's acceptable to set a high standard for yourself, but expecting to master something that requires practice will only deplete your self-esteem. No one expects perfection from a baby as it learns to walk and talk, and yet people hold themselves to an unrealistic standard when they're learning something new. Just because you understand a concept doesn't mean you've mastered its practice. Every single new thing you've learned in your life you followed these steps in the learning curve.

In the early 1960s, three management professors at NYU identified the four stages of learning that define the psychological states involved in the process of progressing from incompetence to competence in a skill: unconscious incompetence, conscious incompetence, conscious competence, and unconscious competence. To understand these four stages, let's use driving a car as an example. When you were a baby, you didn't have any idea you were being driven around in a car by the adults who carried you from place to place (even if you liked the comfortable feeling of the purring engine). This is Unconscious Incompetence: You have no idea that you don't know how to drive the car. As you get older, you become aware that your parents can drive, but you can't, Conscious Incompetence—you're conscious that you don't know how to do that thing. Once you get your learner's permit, with extreme focus and concentration you can drive the car. Conscious Competence—you know how to do it, but you have to consciously focus on the task. Now when you drive the car, you're not thinking about how to do it; you just get in and drive while you're thinking about an issue at work, singing along to a song, eating a sandwich, or putting on lipstick. This is Unconscious Competence—you no longer have to concentrate on the task. It's become an unconscious habit.

Keep the four stages of learning in mind as you practice and become comfortable with the SHYFT and move through the Steps to Emotional Authenticity. Practice. Practice. Practice. And never expect perfection. You'll find that no matter the response, you'll feel better when you speak your truth. This is a key element of dating on purpose: By being authentic, you can evaluate an ideal match through the dating process. You can discover the right match for you by simply observing the other person's capacity when you share your feelings with them. Creating emotional connection is one of the most important skills for sharing your life with a beloved partner. It's crucial that you practice now, *before* you're partnered up. You'll be grateful later on when a difficult situation arises in your relationship, and you've already established great communication with your partner.

Evelyn grew up with a deep-seated fear of rejection. She felt rejected by her mother most of her life, and when she was young, her mother was jealous of Evelyn's relationship with her father. Her mother was also very vocal and overbearing when expressing her emotions, and Evelyn swore she wouldn't be like her mother, so she spent most of her adult life swallowing her feelings and trying to please others. Well into her sixties, she'd been divorced twice and was quite comfortable on her own. She reached out to us because she'd started dating a man she liked a lot but was unsure if he was an ideal match for her long-term. She didn't want to repeat her past mistakes and was determined to break the pattern of choosing emotionally unavailable men.

It was easy to spot Evelyn's habit of people-pleasing, which caused her to keep her feelings to herself. Constantly assuming the man she was dating didn't care about her wants or needs would trigger her to clam up and imagine the worst. The most poignant example happened a couple of weeks before Valentine's Day. Evelyn felt strongly that Valentine's Day was special and hoped that he'd make a grand gesture. Unfortunately, she was reluctant to speak up about her expectations for this romantic holiday, and the more she thought about not having plans on Valentine's Day, the more upset she became. We suggested she share her desires and make a request of him, but even thinking about initiating the conversation caused her to get teary-eyed. Evelyn was convinced she'd spend Valentine's Day alone and she'd once again wasted her time dating a man who couldn't meet her needs. Her disappointment and fear were all inside her mind: she hadn't expressed her desires to him, and Valentine's Day was still a couple of weeks away. We encouraged her to use the SHYFT to let him know it's an important holiday for her and take the risk to share her feelings. Much to her surprise, he was receptive to her feelings and told her he'd been thinking about Valentine's Day and really wanted to spend the day with her and make it special. They ended up having a wonderful day together, her fears about being rejected were just paper tigers, and the strategy of keeping her feelings to herself finally started to fall apart. Over time, Evelyn became accustomed to taking the risk of sharing her feelings as well as making requests. Her relationship with this man blossomed, and she even felt closer to her brother and her children. All her relationships improved simply by speaking her truth. She's now comfortable speaking up and creating connection instead of withdrawing and feeling isolated and alone.

Creating Healthy Boundaries

One of the fallacies of romantic love is that your partner fulfills you in every way, that there shouldn't be any boundaries between the two of you, and that the right person will know what you want without having to ask. The idea that two people who are "meant to be together" merge into one is the recipe for codependency. Just as in the "Jerry Maguire Myth" from the Tom Cruise movie, the idea that someone completes you describes a codependent relationship. A lack of boundaries creates dysfunction and toxicity and can lead to abuse. Respectful love has a boundary. There is a boundary between where Orna ends and Matthew begins and vice versa—that border is filled with respect. Healthy love is interdependent, not codependent.

Boundaries define where you end and your partner begins as well as what is your responsibility and what is your partner's responsibility. They give you guidelines for respectful communication, interaction, and coexistence. The Responsibility Equation makes this boundary crystal clear: **When someone has a problem with you, it's *their* problem. When you have a problem with someone, it's *your* problem.** Relationships are dysfunctional when either partner takes too much responsibility or doesn't take enough responsibility.

The majority of our clients take too much responsibility. They're the peacekeepers in their family, which may spill over at work or even in their group of friends. They worry and fret about how to say or do something, trying as hard as they can to never upset anyone. Walking on eggshells through life is a detriment to your happiness, your peace, and your fulfillment. You're a unique being, and there's no one exactly like you. Just like your fingerprints are unique from nearly eight billion people on the planet, you're the only you there will ever be. It's not your role to shrink so others won't feel uncomfortable around you.

It's not your role to shrink so others won't feel uncomfortable around you.

Knowing how to set and keep healthy boundaries will benefit all of your relationships, including friends, family, lovers, exes, acquaintances, and coworkers, even your boss. Our clients who are givers are relieved when they discover healthy boundaries. They find they have more time for themselves and become much more productive and their lives are much more peaceful.

It's important to find a happy medium with setting boundaries. If you've struggled to set and keep boundaries you may find yourself overcorrecting and setting hard boundaries like the Great Wall of China. Setting boundaries shouldn't be all or nothing. It's not either no boundaries at all or rigid boundaries; there's a lot of gray area, especially with people who've earned the benefit of the doubt.

If you're unsure how to set boundaries, it helps to get clear on where you are in relation to everyone in your life. Imagine you're the bull's eye on a dart board, right in the center, and everyone else in your life is placed on the rings from closest to you to the furthest away from you. Start evaluating people in your life to see where they belong on your dartboard. The people who are supportive of you, believe in your dreams and goals, leave you feeling good about yourself, and who you're able to easily be authentic with are in the ring closest to you. You don't worry about what to say or how to say it with these people. You're relaxed when you're with them. If there's miscommunication or another kind of issue, you can work through it with them fairly easily.

When you're thinking about where to place people on the board, don't automatically put family members in the closest ring. Evaluate each person in your life separately and equally, without taking blood relations into account. Simply observe and evaluate yourself when you interact with them and how they respond to you. Place the people you trust and you're most comfortable with on the innermost ring. When setting boundaries, the people closest to you get the most wiggle room. These people have earned the benefit of the doubt. They can have a bad day, and you can cut them some slack. If you worry about someone's moods, their reactions, their communication, or you don't trust them enough to share your truth, push them to the outer rings of the dart board. When you set boundaries with people on the outer rings, it's okay to be more clear-cut and not give them the benefit of the doubt because they haven't earned it.

As you continue on this journey of speaking up for yourself and sharing your truth, you'll likely have to rearrange people on your dartboard. You may find that people surprise you. Some people will prove themselves to have more capacity than you imagined; maybe they'll be much more caring and compassionate than you thought. And the opposite may occur with other people; they may disappoint you, and you may have to create some distance from them. Your goal is to evaluate each person's capacity so you can find the people who are supportive and get you. They're your tribe, whether you're related to them or not. Finding your tribe is just as important as finding your mate because your life partner won't be everything for you—that's too much pressure and expectation to put on one person. Human beings live in communities so they can look out for one another. Finding the community that accepts you without trying to change you will bring you joy and fulfillment, and this tribe may introduce you to your soulmate.

Practicing the tools in this chapter builds your self-esteem and self-confidence. Expressing how you feel is a way of saying, "I count and I matter; therefore, how I feel matters." You may have a habit of putting your needs and wants aside to get along and avoid conflict. Unfortunately, going along to get along in the dating process will never reveal your soulmate. If all you do is avoid conflict, you'll never find the person who is willing to stand by you. Your beloved will want you to shine your light brightly, and the only way for them to see you and recognize you is to show up and be your authentic unique self. Your beloved will love that thing about you that all the others left you over. It may seem like an impossibility, but it's the truth. The right partner will absolutely adore your unique and special quirks and characteristics. They won't need you to change.

LOVE ON PURPOSE EXERCISE—WORKING OUT AT THE AUTHENTICITY GYM

The Steps to Emotional Authenticity are your marathon training at the authenticity gym. The SHYFT is the tool you're going to practice as you interact with other people. Look over the Steps to Emotional Authenticity to discover which step you struggle with most often, and then stretch out of your comfort zone to master that step. Once you feel confident, add on and practice the following step and continue until you can excel at all five steps.

To begin, practice the SHYFT (Speak How You Feel Template) with the people in your innermost circle. Don't worry about doing it perfectly because you can always clean it up with them. Release any expectation that you will get it right, and remember, we still mess this up ourselves. Part of this exercise is being willing to do it wrong and to have the experience of cleaning your interaction up after the fact. Your goal is to incorporate the Steps to Emotional Authenticity along with the SHYFT into your daily life as a new way of communicating and interacting with all the people in your life. It will also be incorporated into how you communicate while dating in later chapters. These are the foundational tools to master the uncomfortable conversations required for emotional intimacy to thrive and grow year after year, decade after decade.

Write down the Steps to Emotional Authenticity and put the list somewhere you can see it daily to help remind you the importance of authenticity in creating connection. Use your journal to practice writing out your SHYFT communication. After the fact, reflect on how it went. Where could you have been clearer in your communication? What did their reaction teach you about their capacity to hear you and respect your desires? How do you feel having shared your authentic truth and being heard? The more you lean into having the uncomfortable conversations with people in your life, the more comfortable you'll become with setting and keeping boundaries in your relationships.

Scan the QR code for bonus materials and video trainings:

7

Healing Your Heart

*"It is by going down into the abyss that we recover the trea-
sures of life. Where you stumble, there lies your treasure."*
—Joseph Campbell

Elisa had just gone through a difficult divorce. The dissolution of
her marriage served as a constant reminder that she'd messed up
her life yet again. It seemed her broken heart would never heal.
She felt like she was always a disappointment to those she loved,
just like with her father who'd wanted her to be a boy. Feeling
rejected caused Elisa to close off her heart to protect herself from
further sadness and grief. Her lack of confidence kept her away
from dating, closed off from her feelings, and focused on raising
her children. Her skepticism of lasting love was driven by the belief
that no one would ever be supportive of her or stick by her when
life became difficult. Having been raised as if she was a boy, she
felt she could never measure up, and even now as a divorced
mother of two young boys, she felt incompetent. She fought regularly with her ex over their differing parenting styles and felt
defeated by her inability to get him to work with her. With each
one of their interactions, she was on pins and needles, afraid he
would withhold assistance and communication if she didn't
respond exactly as he wished. All these hardships had stripped

her of the vitality she once possessed. Their contentious relationship made it difficult to even consider starting to date again. Still in her early thirties, she didn't want to spend the rest of her life on her own and longed to have a life partner who understood her.

In order to break free from her negative emotional rut and heal her broken heart, Elisa had to accept her faults, celebrate her strengths, learn to set and keep boundaries, and stop taking responsibility for other people's behavior. Ultimately she had to learn from her failed marriage and find gratitude for the experience. She finally relaxed, became less defensive, and stopped taking everything personally. Changing her communication style with her ex by embracing the SHYFT immensely improved their interactions. They got on the same page raising their boys, and she finally felt supported by him instead of feeling all alone. Rather than anger, she finally felt grateful the marriage had ended, and her confidence and self-esteem grew.

With peace in her home life, she rejoined the dating world. Through several short-term relationships the vision of her true soul partnership became crystal clear—she needed someone to be her ally in life—which was the opposite of her love imprint, "I can't count on love." By definition, an ally is someone you can rely on. When Elisa met Glenn online, the start was very different than all of her previous relationships. He was incredibly kind and patient with her, and she felt safe and validated by his calm steady presence. There was one hiccup: Glenn lived in another state several hundred miles away, and his business made relocating impossible for him. Regular video dates and travel became the norm as their budding relationship grew into the vision she had created for her beloved partnership. Eventually, and after practicing her request several dozen times and picking her moment, Elisa asked her ex if she could take the boys to live with Glenn for the summer—to her delight he agreed! That summer set the stage for her and the boys to move in with Glenn permanently. This blended family was not what Elisa had originally envisioned for her life when she became a mother but has become the foundation for her and her family to thrive. She's living life on her terms, and her beloved Glenn is the most supportive and loving man she's ever known.

Breakups are hard; they can be one of the most painful experiences in life. Navigating heartbreak allows you to become more resilient and wiser from your experiences. Heartbreak can be an unexpected teacher, allowing you to grow into a more loving and compassionate person. Without healing your heartache, you can become more cautious with your heart, or even worse, become bitter. The desire to protect your heart doesn't safeguard you from heartbreak or loneliness; instead, it shields you from the love you desire. Additionally, heartbreak is not a sign of failure; rather, it's an opportunity for your heart to break open so you can receive more love. Pour compassion and forgiveness into your broken heart and watch it grow like the Grinch's on Christmas Day. Love requires risk, and the courage to continue to invest your heart despite your disappointments comes when you realize that you can never lose love, because love is your birthright and comes from inside of you.

Midway through our work together, Sonia met Kent, who'd been divorced for less than a year. We advised her to proceed slowly; instead, they quickly went exclusive. For the next year, they navigated conflicts, grew closer, and eventually started discussing moving in together. Sonia believed the relationship was getting stronger between them. They didn't fight, their sex life was thriving, and as far as she could determine there were no issues between them. One night, while discussing the finer details of moving in together, Kent broke down and said, "I can't do this!" He took all his stuff and left without an explanation.

Normally this would have thrown Sonia into a downward spiral of self-recrimination and regret, lamenting what she'd done wrong and blaming herself for the relationship not working out. But this breakup was very different for her. Sonia allowed herself to feel and experience grief, and even though she occasionally went down the rabbit hole of self-pity, she was able to keep her heart open and stay positive and hopeful that she'd find her beloved. She was grateful for Kent because he'd treated her better than anyone she'd ever been with (including her ex-husband). Looking back on their year together, she realized how much she'd progressed and matured. It was clear that Kent hadn't been upfront with her; however, she'd been oblivious to his dodging conflict. Once they were exclusive, she was the one leading the relationship forward, and he would just go along with her. Ultimately, he hadn't been authentic.

These were huge realizations for Sonia. In the past, she would've taken a hundred percent responsibility for the relationship ending, but now she was able to own her mistakes without taking his on. Her other breakups had been devastating for her. They were dramatic emotional experiences that took her many months to recover from. Now she was able to move quickly through her darker moments and still feel hopeful about the future. After dedicating some time to mourn, Sonia was ready to start dating again. Due to her experience with Kent, she was determined to move more slowly through the dating process, not rush to exclusivity, and let guys pursue her. For a while, she set up a dating rotation of several men and ultimately met Clayton. He was smitten with her and wanted to become exclusive immediately. She put on the brakes while also letting him know she was interested in getting to know him *before* going exclusive. Her fear that he would move on to someone else who would commit proved false, and she kept her dating rotation going. The goal was to find out if Clayton was emotionally available for a relationship. Over time, he kept showing up for her, honoring her requests, demonstrating that he was willing to wait for her, and stating that he wanted a long-term relationship. Eventually Sonia let him know she was ready to stop dating other guys, and they discussed the fact that neither of them wanted another marriage. They're still together, and their love grows stronger each year. Taking time through the dating process was the key for Sonia to find her ideal match.

Healing your heart doesn't mean you rush through grief. Despite the negative feelings that come up when you've been hurt, *not* processing them and tuning them out can create a lot more long-term damage to your well-being than *feeling* them ever could. Similarly, letting your heartache harden your heart only hurts you and no one else. Learning to move through heartache and to bounce back from a breakup is essential on the path to long-lasting love.

A breakup can become the impetus for you to change your approach to love by embracing that everything is happening for you, not to you. We believe that life constantly presents you with situations that challenge you to grow into a better version of yourself. Your soul manifests in the physical world of polarity to experience the friction of life and evolve through strife. You don't have to believe in a soul to use your breakups as fuel to become a better person. Whatever you do or do not believe in, God, Jesus, Moses, Allah, Science, The Universe, or even the Great Spaghetti

A breakup can become the impetus for you to change your approach to love by embracing that everything is happening for you, not to you.

Monster, or whatever you call that force greater than yourself, when you approach the events in your life with an open mind and curiosity, you can learn from all your experiences and grow. Our dear friend and motivational speaker Les Brown says, "People come into your life for a reason, a season, or a lifetime." Finding the reason a person who broke your heart came into your life allows you to access gratitude for the experience. What if your ex came into your life so you could heal your wounds and prepare you for a beloved relationship? What if they showed up to make you a better person? Instead of becoming bitter about love, you can find gratitude for your ex because they inspired you to grow and prepare for a lasting loving partnership.

The Golden Nugget of Learning: Five Steps to Getting Over Heartbreak

Whether the heartbreak is fresh and you're still feeling raw, or the heartbreak happened years ago and you're still carrying a torch for the one that got away, the "Golden Nugget of Learning" guides you to discover the reason the person who broke your heart came into your life and opens the door to gratitude for the experience despite the pain of the loss. It may seem daunting to think that you could be grateful for someone who broke your heart, but by embracing each step you'll inevitably find your way there.

Step One: Feel All of Your Feelings

It may seem counterintuitive because the pain of heartbreak can be intense, but the only way to release the pain is to go through it to the other side. Rather than going numb or attempting to shove down all those icky emotions—feel all of your feelings.

There's no shortcut to skirt around your negative emotions, and ultimately, we're saving you precious time, because what you resist will persist. Allow your feelings to move through you, letting each difficult emotion come up, be expressed, and create space for the next emotion. Remember, your feelings are like ocean waves crashing to the shore.

Just like not getting a job you really wanted, a breakup is a loss. Remind your brain that you've been through other losses and recovered. The pain you're feeling is a natural response, and it's temporary. You had hope that your relationship would last, and it's appropriate to mourn the loss of the future life you thought you'd have. Now your life is changing, and you're moving in a new direction. Begin the healing process by referring to the relationship in the past tense. The two of you *were* partners, and you *used to* be together. Like ripping off a band-aid quickly, the sooner you do this, the faster you'll feel better overall. Book time in your calendar to grieve and mourn the loss. Put on sad songs or a sad movie and cry your eyes out. The only way out of your current state is to go through the emotions. Feeling better will happen faster when you commit to the experience of your negative emotions.

While experiencing your emotions, do your best not to indulge in the emotional stories attached to them. As we stated before, your mind is looking for meaning in your emotional experiences, and the meanings you create influence how you see the world. Here's how to avoid creating meanings that keep you stuck. Express the sadness, but don't wallow in the belief that no one will ever love you again. State your anger, but don't tell yourself that all men or all women can't be trusted. Convey your hurt and share it, but don't succumb to the false belief that love has passed you by. Breakups are a part of life; by feeling your feelings, you move the emotional energy through your body and release it. Remember, your emotions are temporary, and when you attach meaning to them you create an emotional story that makes them appear more permanent. Detach from the story in your mind; simply focus on body sensations so your emotions can move through you more quickly. Stay out of your head and the meanings your mind wants to attach to your emotions. Just be with the emotion without having to do anything with it.

Step Two: Don't Rush to Forgiveness

There's a time for forgiveness after a breakup, but don't hurry to get there. Forgiveness is an important step to healing your heart, and when you're ready to forgive, it opens your heart to compassion and creates space for love. However, forgiveness can only come into play once you've truly mourned, grieved, and given up the hope that they'll come back to you. Forgiving too quickly can be a way of spiritual bypassing, using a spiritual practice as a defense mechanism or shield. If the idea of forgiveness comes to you too quickly, move it to the back burner and instead entertain the thoughts in your head about your ex. Get all those negative thoughts out of your system. You don't want to gloss over a breakup and leave it to fester to create problems in your next relationship. You can wish for something bad to happen to them; it's okay. Thinking wicked thoughts does not make you a bad person—just don't take any action on those thoughts.

There's no time limit on grief; it may sneak up on you at any time or place. Your healing is not on a linear path, so be okay with the fits and starts. You may end up doing the Cha-Cha, two steps forward, one step back. Think of it as dancing with yourself to create a new relationship with the most important person in your life—*You!*

Step Three: Kill the Hope

Hope is the first thing that enters a relationship, and it's the last thing to leave. Once you've moved through the first two steps, it's time for your hope of reconciliation to die. You may recoil at the thought of killing the hope, but you're stronger than you think, and any sliver of hope will prolong your pain. Slaying the hope frees up your energy and sets up healing so you can move on. Killing the hope that circum- stances will be different is one of the most pow- erful steps you can take after a breakup. As long as there's hope, you'll settle for crumbs. You'll see any positive interaction with your ex as a signal that maybe, just maybe, the two of you will get back together. Holding on to hope will keep you stuck, allow your broken heart to fester, and block love from anyone else because there's no space for them in your heart.

> *Hope is the first thing that enters a relationship, and it's the last thing to leave.*

Part of killing the hope is to avoid offering or accepting friendship as a consolation prize. A friend is someone you'd want to introduce to your future soulmate and invite to your wedding someday. Is your ex on that list? People offer friendship after a breakup because they don't want to hurt you and they feel guilty for ending the relationship. But that offer can lead to an imbal- anced relationship that leaves the broken-hearted scrambling for clues that their ex might want them back. An offer of friend- ship keeps hope alive, and that hope will never be fulfilled, so kindly and firmly reject their offer to be friends. This doesn't mean you can't be friendly if you run into each other, but there's a big distinction between being friendly with someone you used to date and being friends with an ex. You can end up being friends with an ex after you've both moved on and healed. It's not something you have to fret about in the moments after you've broken up; instead, focus on moving through your healing journey.

Step Four: Set Clear Boundaries

Taking steps that move you toward healing your heart allows you to release your ex and move on. One of those is to set a communication boundary. By setting a clear boundary, you're exercising the right to protect yourself. Setting boundaries is also an act of self-care. Your heartache is a wound that requires healing. Every time you have contact with your ex, it's like tearing off a scab on a wound, slowing down the healing process.

One important acronym that might help you determine the right kind of boundary to set is NRN (No Response Necessary). Unwanted texts, phone calls, and emails do not need to be responded to. There's no need to respond immediately if your ex does contact you. Wait before you say or do something that will re-engage the two of you. Most situations do not require your immediate response, and many require no response at all.

You may want to make a clear request that your ex does not contact you in any way. This gives you the gift of space and time so that you can process the separation, grieve, and move on. Limiting contact like this includes virtually too, so it's best to block them on all social media platforms. Avoid their local hangouts, and make a point of not driving by their home or workplace. Change their name in your phone to "Do Not

Answer," because you'll always follow this direction from yourself. Don't just delete their contact record. Your subconscious mind will highlight everything familiar, and whether or not you think you know their phone number—you don't want to take that chance.

If you can delegate necessary contact to a third party, then do so. Collecting your personal items and giving your ex their items can be done this way. If you coparent with your ex, you may need to have contact. Dealing with a joint business or settling finances may also require you to communicate with your ex. Limit all communication to the absolute necessities. Avoid rehashing the relationship with them. It may feel cathartic to vent your hurt and frustration, but it will keep you stuck in your old dynamic. Create as much physical and emotional space as you need to protect your vulnerable heart. Setting yourself up for healing success will ensure you feel better ASAP.

Step Five: Find the Golden Nugget of Learning

Now you're ready to look for the golden nugget—the reason this person came into your life and the lesson they showed up to teach you. You'll know you've uncovered the golden nugget when you feel grateful for the whole experience and any regrets have melted away. The golden nugget could reveal a pattern you want to break—for example, "I learned how to identify toxic people; now I want to steer clear of them." Or "I no longer want to date emotionally unavailable partners." The most effective golden nuggets are the ones that reveal something you still need to master, like improving your communication skills or speaking up for yourself. Maybe you realize that you have a habit of going into sacrifice and you vow to put your needs first.

Begin by freewriting about the relationship and all the insights you have looking back on the time you spent together. This exercise is best with pen to paper and not on a digital device. Journal your feelings and thoughts about what was familiar and also what was different about yourself in this relationship. You've discovered the golden nugget when you feel grateful for the whole experience of having had the relationship so you can become a better, more evolved version of yourself. Once you mine the relationship for the golden nugget, you'll no longer pine for your ex because the attachment to the relationship will be severed.

Now you're ready to let your ex go for good. Write them a letter of gratitude that you'll never send. This ritual sets your heart free, allows you to forgive what occurred between the two of you, and clears the way for you to love again and to be wiser and better for the experience. This letter is for you (not for your ex), so as tempting as it may be to send it—*don't*. You can start with this phrase: "I'm so grateful you came into my life, because without you I never would have discovered . . ." [fill in the blank]. When you're done writing the letter, put it aside for a couple of days. Then come back to it and see if there are any edits you'd like to make. When you feel it's complete, implement this ritual:

1. Read the letter out loud.
2. Say out loud, "I release this for the highest good of all."
3. Then burn the letter.

You can burn it in your fireplace, outside in a fire pit, or even in your kitchen sink. As the letter burns, visualize the energetic ties between you disappearing. Imagine you've moved closer to the best version of yourself due to the relationship. Do not keep a copy of the letter. Fire is a purifying energy, and by burning it you're breaking the connection to your ex. Now that you've received the learning, there's no need to keep the letter; burn it and let the relationship go. Trust that by doing this exercise you've received the benefits required to move on. The Golden Nugget of Learning allows you to look at life like a gameboard. The emotional investment you made to partner with someone garnered a return, and the profit is your own growth.

Decades ago, Orna reconnected with Jim, an acquaintance from college, and they started a relationship that lasted nearly a year. Soon after their breakup, Orna began the golden nugget exercise to figure out why this relationship came into her life. What did Jim show up to teach her or show her? This time it was more difficult to figure out. She had initiated the breakup, so Orna thought that was why she was struggling to find the goodies. After weeks of introspection and journaling, the revelation came: Jim's family loved each other respectfully. In Orna's upbringing, there were no boundaries; if someone said, "I love you," that meant that they could do anything to you—including beat and berate you. The purpose of the relationship with Jim was to highlight respectful love. If Orna wanted to be loved respectfully, she had to first learn to set and keep healthy boundaries. The affirmation, "The men I love are loving me respectfully," was born that day. This priceless lesson came from the grief of heartbreak.

You can find golden nuggets, goodies, and growth from every relationship that didn't last. And then some relationships transform you forever because they prepare you for your beloved in a very specific way. These partners show up as if they are the very thing you've been hoping and praying for only to turn out to be Your Love Imprint match—a match to your childhood wound.

These alchemizing relationships are what we refer to as a "Threshold Guardian." These lovers are like the gatekeepers you have to get past in a video game before you can move up to the next level. On your journey to lasting love, the next level is your soulmate relationship.

This is what happened to Justin, who was thrilled that he'd finally met the perfect woman. Ingrid was smart, successful, and sophisticated, and they had great chemistry. He was frustrated with dating because a lot of the women he met were more interested in him than he was in them. Upon meeting Ingrid, it just clicked, and the internal signal he'd always interpreted as meeting "The One" occurred. The relationship was progressing well, but something wasn't right. When he told her he loved her for the first time she replied with, "Thanks for telling me." His anxiety hit new levels, and his insecurity ultimately pushed Ingrid away. Digging deeper into his initial excitement as well as his forthcoming anxiety and insecurity, we realized that Ingrid was a love imprint match for Justin. She was an energetic match to his childhood story of "I'm not worthy of the love I want." Suddenly, a realization struck Justin like a lightning bolt. "Oh, you mean that feeling of excitement isn't what I'm actually looking for?"

The realization that his love imprint had steered him right to the rejection and disappointment he'd felt as a boy was viscerally present. "Oh right, it's a familiar signal," he said to us. Now he was ready to let go of his unrealistic expectations of a partner and be open to experiencing something brand new. Ingrid showed up to reveal the final puzzle piece to break his negative pattern in love. Justin felt a bit silly admitting that he was addicted to the rush he'd been looking for and lamented all the women he'd passed over who didn't give him that thrilling sensation. When we asked him how that excitement felt in his body and if it was comfortable and relaxing, he laughed—it was the opposite. No wonder lasting love had been so elusive!

Despite our best efforts to explain to Justin that a love imprint match is a match to his childhood wound, the experience of going through the negative pattern one more time locked it in forever. Just like riding a bike, once you learn to balance it, you can't unlearn it. Once the spell of his love imprint was broken, Justin would never allow it to take hold of his heart again. With his newfound freedom of choice, he was able to cultivate discernment through the dating process to find an ideal match. His beloved partnership is stable, calm, and brings him a sense of inner peace. The feelings of anxiety and uncertainty that he mistook for excitement were never part of their connection from the start.

In *The Hero's Journey*, Joseph Campbell explains the role of the Threshold Guardian as an archetypal character who stands between the hero and their goal. To continue their journey, the hero must defeat the Threshold Guardian and open the portal to another world. Threshold Guardian relationships are the ones that tempt you to stay stuck in your negative pattern. Their familiarity is part of their appeal. On the surface, you think you're in brand new territory, and the rush of good feelings that are familiar are incredibly seductive. The moment it's revealed to be a familiar experience, you must end the relationship, break the cycle, and move on. It's a test that you must pass to get the long-lasting love you desire. Justin passed his test when he finally understood the difference between a love imprint match and a soulmate connection. Your Love Imprint strategies can be hard to recognize because in the delusion of excitement it's easy to ignore that the signal is really saying, "This is familiar! This is familiar!"

Jim revealed to Orna that respectful love was a key ingredient for her vision of a soulmate relationship, and she needed to learn to love respectfully. When Matthew realized that Sarah was mirroring his lack of self-acceptance, and he made the choice to move on, cultivate that aspect of himself, and slayed his Threshold Guardian, it opened the door to meet Orna.

You may be closer than you realize to your goal. Recognize the familiar excitement of Your Love Imprint patterns and say, "No" to anything less than what you truly desire and deserve. These examples illustrate opportunities for emotional growth and more evolved relationship skills. Golden nuggets can be unearthed because of a painful experience and can also be found when you date someone who treats you better than any of your previous partners. An ex doesn't have to be "The One" to hone the vision of your ideal romantic partnership. The key to finding the golden nugget is to ask yourself, "Why did it have to be this person?" It's not something you would have figured out on your own with a different partner. Why did *this particular person* show up in your life? What did they come into your life to teach you or to show you?

LOVE ON PURPOSE EXERCISES

A broken heart is the source of a great deal of blocks to love. When left unhealed, it can close your heart to love, leave you feeling hopeless, and even worse leave you feeling cynical. The following exercises will guide you to healing your heart and creating space for love.

The Golden Nugget of Learning

To discover the Golden Nugget of Learning, first review the five steps outlined in this chapter and then set aside time to journal about your last relationship (or the one that you can't stop thinking about). Simply freewrite whatever comes to mind. Don't limit yourself and don't edit yourself. Allow your thoughts and feelings to flow and see what shows up. Here are some prompts to help you get started:

1. Instead of focusing on what didn't work or the regrets you may have about the relationship, look at the dynamic between the two of you from a different point of view. Make a distinction between which patterns were a repeat of past relationships and what may have been new and not familiar about this particular relationship.

2. Write down what you've learned or what you need to learn to approach love differently next time. See if there are any negative patterns you can identify or if there are any relationship skills you need to develop. You can also list how this relationship was different in a positive way from your past relationships. You may find large nuggets that can transform your future relationships, and small nuggets that provide flashes of insight.

You don't have to limit yourself to a specific number of insights. One big golden nugget can be just as valuable as three or four little ones. When you're done, read through your thoughts and look for the golden nugget that lights you up and triggers a feeling of gratitude for the experience. Look for your big aha moments. Once you've zeroed in on what your ex showed up to teach you about love, write the letter of gratitude that you'll never send. Complete the ritual and release them for good by burning the letter. You can separately complete this exercise with any past significant partners you've had. Don't rush through this process, as you may need some time in between the steps, and be sure to leave a couple of weeks minimum in between different exes. You've got this!

Ho'oponopono—Healing Your Heart with Forgiveness

Ho'oponopono is the Hawaiian spiritual practice of forgiveness and reconciliation. "Pono," means integrity in Hawaiian. Ho'oponopono means to come back into integrity with yourself, setting things right, or putting things back in order. This ancient Hawaiian practice is a process of coming back into integrity with yourself. It's one of the most powerful tools for practicing forgiveness and releasing the past. When you have mixed emotions around what you desire because subconsciously you're conflicted, your actions are out of integrity with your desires. Ho'oponopono can bring you back into integrity with yourself and release your fear, anger, sadness, hurt, shame, and guilt over your past experiences.

There are four steps to the Ho'oponopono practice after you've selected a person you wish to forgive (that person can be yourself).

1. Repentance: Acknowledge your part in the situation. Say aloud to yourself, "I'm sorry."
2. Forgiveness: Ask for forgiveness. Say, "Please forgive me."
3. Gratitude: Express gratitude. Say, "Thank you."
4. Love: Finally, express love and appreciation. Say, "I love you."

This practice releases negative emotions from your past relationship experiences and frees your heart to allow love to manifest more easily and effortlessly. This process does not require you to ever speak to anyone who hurt you in the past or to forget what happened to you. Ho'oponopono releases you from the energetic dance of the past so you can create from a clean slate. First, place your hands over your heart one on top of the other. Then visualize the person you wish to forgive or yourself (it can be a younger version of you). Repeat these phrases over and over as you expand the feeling of love and connection inside of you:

"I'm sorry."

"Please forgive me."

"Thank you."

"I love you."

Repeat for 5–10 minutes.

Practice twice daily until that person or event no longer has a negative charge.

Scan the QR code for bonus materials and video trainings:

8

Fill Your Cup to Overflowing

"Discovering the truth about ourselves is a lifetime's work, but it's worth the effort."

—Fred Rogers

Adelaide was devastated after a brief two-month stint with a guy who professed his love for her on their first date. She seemed flummoxed as to why things had gone wrong. It didn't take us very long to realize she had a habit of self-abandonment, or setting aside her own feelings, desires, and needs for the needs and desires of another person, abandoning herself at the first sign of attraction. She was easily swept off her feet and often got caught up in a fantasy of love at first sight. In the case of this short relationship, she had committed her heart without ever evaluating the capacity of the handsome stranger she'd just met.

A habit of self-abandonment is created when someone is out of rapport with their emotional life and expects someone else to make them feel better and take care of their needs. Adelaide's self-abandonment strategy came from her fear of abandonment and being left behind. As an attractive woman by any standard, Adelaide's good looks were wreaking havoc in her love life. Society assumes that attractive people have it easy when it comes to love (another myth we like to bust). Once she was under the spell of a guy promising her the moon, Adelaide seemed to have no brains to evaluate whether he was a good long-term match for her. Her habit of self-abandonment had her on an emotional rollercoaster through the dating process, riding waves of hope, to excitement, to disappointment. The impulse to fantasize and imagine a future with a stranger stemmed from her love imprint, "I'm not enough," creating profound sadness from this core wound. Her fantasizing and futurizing would begin at initial contact through an app, often before she had ever met him in person.

Adelaide's behavior may sound extreme to you, but it's wildly common for people to imagine coupling with someone before ever meeting them, and certainly before knowing if that person is capable of meeting their needs. That's because hope is the first thing that comes into a relationship and it's the last thing to leave. Rather than being grounded in her sense of self, Adelaide was like an emotional plastic bag blowing in the wind, looking for something to grab ahold of. The profound sadness from her core wound caused her to merge as quickly as possible to feel connected to another person. Merging is an immature connection to another person fueled by fear of separation. This ultimately creates a relationship with no boundaries.

The ideas put into Adelaide's head from songs, poems, movies, and books created a fantasy of how love should show up and what it's supposed to feel like. The desire for love to magically appear outside of her when it was lacking inside of her was the real issue. Rather than obsessively imagining a future with a stranger, we asked Adelaide to put her own desires first and to connect with the little girl inside of her. Creating a new relationship with herself was imperative to end her cycle of self-abandonment.

Years ago, Orna stepped up to the counter at a coffeehouse where she was meeting a date. She placed her order for a chai latte with almond milk and then looked around at the people seated on the back patio. There was one guy out there who kind of resembled the guy from JDate—only if the photo he posted was taken a decade earlier, and by far the best photo this guy had ever taken in his life. When her order came up, she confidently walked to the back and sat down. She knew her profile photo was current and looked exactly as she appeared in real life, so if that guy was him, he'd have to come to her. Much to her chagrin, even before her tush was comfortably in the seat, he was already making a beeline for her. "Are you Orna?" asked this schleppy guy who sheepishly started asking questions about a producer she'd worked for in the film industry. In less than five minutes, Orna stood up and stated, "I didn't think this was a job interview, I'm leaving." Before he could finish saying he'd googled her, she was out the exit.

Walking down Main Street, she caught her reflection in one of the storefront windows, and a broad smile sprang on her face. For the first time in her life she didn't sacrifice her happiness for someone else's comfort. She wasn't rude; she'd taken care of herself and spoken her mind. "I've arrived! I'm finally the woman I've always wanted to be," she thought to herself. From the reflection staring back at her she looked good, she felt good, and looked oddly taller than ever before. "Maybe this is what it feels like to love yourself?" she said. She was so proud that she didn't allow her time to be wasted under false pretense. At last she'd let go of the habit of abandoning her wants and needs to defer to the guy across the table.

The most important relationship you'll ever have is the one you have with yourself, yet when you hear the words "self-love," or when someone suggests that you "love yourself," it's difficult to know exactly what to do. Loving yourself means you treat yourself as worthy of being loved. You do this by being kind and compassionate with yourself. Only by embracing the truth *that you are worth loving* can you be open to receive love from another.

Ultimately, the love you seek is inside of you, and when you connect with your beloved, the love you have for yourself will be reflected back to you in their eyes. If you don't believe you're worthy of love, you won't be able to accept it from someone else. It'll be an energetic mismatch; it'll feel off like their intentions are false. You might not be able to find a person who's interested in you attractive; you could reject them, unable to receive their affection because it won't feel right. Loving yourself comes from knowing your own value, that you're the prize, and someone must work to prove their worthiness before you invest your heart. When you realize that love comes from inside of you, then you'll never worry about losing love. To come into alignment with the universal truth that you're worth loving, you'll have to take loving actions, have loving thoughts, and feel loving feelings for yourself.

We believe that loving someone means you'll treat them the way *they* want to be treated. The idea that you should treat others the way *you* want to be treated is misguided in intimate relationships. It's useful on a grand scale for how to treat your neighbors and the strangers you meet, but it isn't helpful in your romantic relationship. So when thinking about what it means to love yourself, ask yourself: How do *you* want to be treated by a lover? A friend? A parent? A coworker? A boss? There's likely a throughline in how you'd like to be treated by everyone in your life. Perhaps it's respect? Respectful love has a boundary (as we've already shared with you), but do you love yourself respectfully? Perhaps it's kindness and

Speak to yourself like someone you love.

compassion? Learn to shower yourself with the love you desire from someone else. Most importantly, speak to yourself like someone you love.

Breaking your habit of self-abandonment, which is most likely a strategy tied to Your Love Imprint, requires you to heal the core wounds from childhood. Reconnecting with your inner child and showing your inner child that they count and matter, that their feelings matter and are valid, that they are loved and safe, and that you will love them no matter what helps you reclaim yourself and reparent your inner child. This is the process of filling your cup first and then being of service from your overflow. To discover if self-abandonment is a problem for you, complete the Self-Abandonment Assessment at the end of this chapter.

Healing Your Inner Child

Perhaps growing up, you adopted the idea that you're incomplete until you're partnered up, that until you have a partner you can't go on that trip, sign up for that class, go eat at that new fancy restaurant, or start a new self-improvement program. None of these actions require you to be in partnership; only your limited thinking and your childhood wounding has you putting off these types of activities. Whether you embraced the same values as your family of origin or you rebelled against them, you're still in reaction to what was engendered in your childhood home. Remember, you made these decisions long before you knew who you were and how the world works.

The relationship between you and your parent(s) is an imbalanced relationship because they were fully formed when you came into the world. You were not formed at all. Their fingerprints are all over you, and your need to feel loved and safe drove you to create meaning from their behavior, whether it was helpful or hurtful, loving or indifferent. This is true for anyone who was your caregiver from birth until eight or nine years old and is the basis for Your Love Imprint. These unresolved emotional wounds from childhood (even the "normal" ones) have caused you to lose touch with your inner child (your childlike self that lives in your subconscious and embodies your childhood wounds as well as your innocence, joy, wonder, and imagination from your original, true self). You could say that parts of you splintered off and you rejected them because it was more important to have a connection with a parent or primary caregiver. You may have repressed the desire to make yourself happy and prioritized the happiness of a parent—this is how a strategy of self-abandonment begins. These parts of you still exist today; however, you're alienated from them—it's like being in a cold war with parts of yourself.

Often within the parent–child relationship there's an unspoken contract that's created, and these agreements are hidden blocks to lasting love. Contracts of this nature vary from person to person, and not everyone will have one. In cases of parental alienation, when one parent wrongfully keeps the child from the other parent, it's common for the child to have an issue with the entire gender of the alienated parent. This is not conscious. Additionally, pacts with a parent can begin with the child hearing biased advice over and over again as in, "You can't trust anyone to take care of you," or, "All men will cheat," and also, "Women only marry a wealthy man." An unconscious agreement can also begin with parentification, when a parent uses their child as an emotional or practical support, like a confidant.

This was the case with our client Jacob, whose father deserted the family when he was a baby, leaving his mother to raise him and his older brother. Being the younger child, he had a deep bond with his mother who used him for emotional support, sharing with him things that would have been better suited for a therapist, friend, or adult family member. His entire life, he heard his mother say, "Good men stay, only bad men leave." Jacob came to us wanting to end his engagement to a woman who was emotionally and physically abusive. They were caught in a classic abuse cycle of apology to reconciliation, followed by escalating tension and violent outbursts. She had crossed the line with him on several occasions, and he left to protect himself, staying away for only a couple nights.

Jacob was an accountant and the head of his own firm. He was a very stable man, responsible, caring, and accomplished. Yet whenever he thought of ending this relationship, he felt frozen, and he didn't understand why he couldn't extricate himself from this toxic situation. He was stuck between a rock and a hard place when the obvious answer was to end the relationship. Through our work together we uncovered his unconscious contract with his mother: "To be a good man, a man must stay. Only bad men leave." Just discovering the language of the unconscious contract he had made as a young boy with his mother diminished its hold on him considerably. With our continued support he was able to end the engagement, extricate himself from the relationship, and successfully take all of his belongings with him, having no reason to interact with her again. He's now married to a wonderful woman who's kind and supportive and who treats him with respect.

> A habit of self-abandonment goes hand in hand with the second greatest myth about love—that love requires sacrifice.

A habit of self-abandonment goes hand in hand with the second greatest myth about love—that love requires sacrifice. This isn't true for every kind of love. A parent's job is to take care of their children, and raising them will likely require sacrifice. Dedicating your life in spiritual service to others is choosing a life of sacrifice. However, love between two adults does not require you to sacrifice your needs. In a healthy romantic partnership, your needs will be met most of the time along with some of your wants. If you have a pattern of abandoning yourself to merge with a partner, then you're out of rapport with yourself. The most obvious sign that you're out of rapport with yourself is engaging in self-sabotaging behavior. Some of our clients come to us wondering if deep down they don't want to have a life partner because they sabotage their relationships. These ruinous behaviors are the inner child acting out because they aren't getting the love and attention they require. In order to select an ideal life partner, you must be in rapport with yourself first, and that requires you to repair the relationship with your inner child.

We have created a weekly ritual called "Inner Child Dates" to help repair the relationship with your inner child. Once a week for two to three hours, engage in an activity selected by the little child inside of you. Imagine they are four to seven years old. The goal is to be in discovery of that little child. How do they feel about your relationship? Can they trust you? Do they want more of your attention? Are they craving your love and approval? Ideally, you'll want to schedule the time on your calendar in advance with the activity. This gives your inner child something to look forward to.

This activity is done by yourself and for yourself only. Remove all distractions. To start, for twelve consecutive weeks, choose unique activities. At the end of twelve weeks, reflect on which activities refueled you the most and continue your weekly dates. These dates should be a top priority and treated as if they are the most important event scheduled on your calendar with the most important person. In order to repair your relationship with your inner child, you must re-establish trust with that part of yourself. Being consistent and sticking to your commitment to yourself is an essential component for rebuilding trust. It's good practice to only cancel a date with your inner child when there's an actual emergency. An actual emergency means you had to interact with a doctor, a policeman, or a fireman. If you didn't interact with one these three types of people, then it's not a genuine emergency. If you have an actual emergency, have a talk with your inner child and reschedule it ASAP.

Hosting a weekly Inner Child Date is the remedy for breaking your habit of self-abandonment. This weekly ritual also heals burnout, blocked creativity, resentment, and stress, as well as ending self-sabotage for good. Even if you don't identify with self-abandonment or the urge to merge, take on the challenge of this exercise, because anyone who feels overburdened, disconnected from self, time-challenged, or overworked will benefit. It's also integral to healing the wound of Your Love Imprint and reparenting yourself. Your number one priority in life is to take care of yourself. Learning to fill your own cup not just to full but to overflowing is the key to fulfillment and satisfaction in life. Being of service is its own reward. If you're giving in order to get, you're not being of service. What's in your cup is for you, so if your cup is empty you cannot be of service until you have reserves in your overflow (the saucer). Never let anyone drink from your cup; if you do, you've gone into sacrifice. Weekly Inner Child Dates lead you on a discovery of how to fill your own cup. Taking time to connect with the child inside of you and discovering activities that fill your cup is akin to knowing how to refuel yourself.

Committing to weekly Inner Child Dates is the path to bring together all the parts of you that splintered off in childhood and to get back in rapport with yourself. This weekly ritual is a reparenting exercise that allows you to heal your relationship with yourself and reintegrate the disconnected parts of you. Self-sacrifice is draining and can trigger depression, or feelings of apathy and hopelessness. During the preflight talk by a flight attendant you're told, "Should the cabin lose pressure, oxygen masks will drop from the overhead area. If you're with someone who needs assistance, please put your own mask on first." If you can't breathe, you can't help someone else breathe.

This practice of self-love helps heal the destructive patterns of self-abandonment and merging, and you'll also discover truths about yourself that will surprise and inspire you—like our client Lisa, who discovered that her inner child was furious with her and didn't trust her. Growing up, she never got the gifts she asked for, and her parents always told her the price for the gifts they gave her. This wounded part of her was angry because as a child she never got what she wanted. During a bonding exercise with her inner child, Lisa went to a candy store and asked the little girl inside her to choose anything she wanted. A voice in her head replied, "What are you trying to do, bribe me?" Lisa worried she had done the Inner Child Date incorrectly; instead, she had discovered valuable information about the state of her relationship with herself and her feelings of worthiness. Your Inner Child Dates may not always be fun; however, they'll always be enlightening. Commit to discover the status of your relationship with your inner child, and it's impossible to do this exercise improperly.

Reparenting is an essential part of the healing process and the journey to lasting love because you can only give others what you've practiced giving yourself. If you weren't loved as you would have liked as a child, learning to love yourself sets the stage to share your life with your beloved. By reparenting yourself and creating a new relationship with your inner child, you're able to get into rapport with yourself, allowing you to stop seeking partners that match Your Love Imprint. You'll also be able to evaluate an ideal match from a new perspective. Improving your relationship with yourself creates an inner transformation that changes your outer experiences, including your behavior and interactions through the dating process. Simply put, when you change the world around you changes.

Inner Child Dates aren't something you do for a few weeks and then never think about again. You don't question if you should eat a few times a day or get a good night's sleep. Self-care is essential on the journey to your beloved, and it must continue even after you're partnered up. Lisa still goes on weekly Inner Child Dates many years into her marriage. When you know how to take care of yourself, your basic needs will be met and the foundation of loving yourself is satisfied. You'll no longer feel the urge to abandon yourself, and you'll be ready to create a healthy, long-lasting partnership.

The bad math of rom-coms is that one plus one equals one. This dynamic creates a dysfunctional, codependent relationship. Our bad math of a healthy relationship is when two whole people come together to create a third entity—the relationship. Each person makes deposits and withdrawals from the partnership. You can think of it like being in a rowboat with your beloved. Sometimes you're both rowing the boat, sometimes you're the only one rowing, sometimes your partner is rowing, and there are also times neither of you is rowing and you're both

A healthy relationship is when two whole people come together to create a third entity—the relationship.

chilling in the boat. Ideally, there's a balance between these four options over a long period of time so no one feels resentful.

Make your Inner Child Dates easy. You can select an activity from one of the sixty we've included below, or you can choose your own. Tap into your creativity and make your best efforts to have fun and discover about yourself. It's not required for you to go out in public and behave like a child. You can do all your activities in the comfort of your own home if you wish. It's also not required that you travel to a particular location you used to go to as a child or recreate some event from childhood. It's important to distinguish self-care activities from an Inner Child Date. Your self-care is always important, but not all self-care activities are a date with your inner child. For example, walking is not an Inner Child Date; that's why you see strollers all over town for people with children—they don't like to walk. Walking is an adult activity; children explore. If you wish to go exploring, that could be an Inner Child Date.

An Inner Child Date is one you do all by yourself, so don't go with a friend, because a friend will distract you from your connection with yourself. If you have a dog and you usually take your dog for a walk, that's not an Inner Child Date. You're shortchanging yourself and your inner child by doing something you'd be doing anyway and calling it an Inner Child Date. If you played with your dog as a child, taking your dog to the dog park and playing could qualify. Going to a class with a bunch of adults is not an Inner Child Date. It may be refueling and fun, but it doesn't help you connect with your inner child.

One of our clients had a childhood illness and she never played outside, and she never learned to ride a bike. She told us she didn't like to play outside because she never did. After several weeks of scheduling Inner Child Dates with herself, she ventured out and rented roller skates. At the start of her next session she shared, "I *love* to play outside!" Another client knew she had a very busy work week ahead, so she got up a few hours earlier than usual and watched cartoons while eating Coco Puffs for breakfast.

In order to have the long-lasting, soul-satisfying love you desire, you must make your happiness a priority. It may seem counterintuitive that by giving your desires precedence you'll find your life partner faster, but by walking this path ourselves, along with thousands of our clients, we can assure you this is one hundred percent True (with a capital T). We ask that you commit to the process and run the experiment, and please play full out!

LOVE ON PURPOSE EXERCISES

How do you know if self-abandonment is an issue for you? This first exercise is an assessment to help you understand how the issue manifests and whether it's something you need to address. If you answer "Yes" to three to five questions, you possibly have an issue with self-abandonment. If you answer "Yes" to more than five, then you have a habit of self-sacrifice in your relationships. In the second exercise, you'll also discover sixty no-cost ideas for Inner Child Dates to make it easy for you to begin the practice.

Self-Abandonment Assessment

Read each of the following questions and circle yes or no next to each question.

In the past, have you sacrificed your own needs to merge with a significant other? YES NO

Do your friends and family complain that you disappear when you're in a relationship? YES NO

Have you stopped your regular self-care activities in order to keep your partner happy? YES NO

Do you regularly give in to your partner's desires even though you don't agree? YES NO

Do you believe that love has to be earned and so you're constantly proving to your partner that you're worth loving? YES NO

Do you feel angry and resentful that you rarely get what you want in your relationships? YES NO

Do you hold onto your frustrations until they build up so much pressure that you explode and then feel regret about your communication? YES NO

Does your fear of being alone cause you to jump into a relationship with the first person who shows interest, even though they're not a good match? YES NO

Is it difficult for you to say "No" to the people you care about? YES NO

Do you seek validation from others for your thoughts, feelings, or opinions? YES NO

Do you keep your desires to yourself and feel resentful that your partner doesn't know what you need? YES NO

Have you set your goals so far out of reach that you fall short only to repeat a cycle of disappointment in yourself? YES NO

Have you felt like no matter how much you gave, it was never enough? YES NO

Do you say "Yes" to other's requests and then regret that you agreed to something you didn't have the time or energy for? YES NO

Are you uncomfortable being alone and therefore constantly jump from one relationship to the next? YES NO

Have you abandoned your values to avoid conflict? YES NO

Do you beat yourself up when you don't meet your high standards for yourself and yet easily forgive others when they make a mistake? YES NO

Do you easily adapt to others to fit in and rarely share your true thoughts or feelings? YES NO

Do you let other people take advantage of you for fear of offending them or having them reject you? YES NO

Do you diminish your upset or answer, "I'm fine" when you're not? YES NO

Sixty Ideas for Low-Cost to No-Cost Inner Child Dates

Draw with crayons.

Make paper airplanes and fly them.

Spend time exploring nature—beach, mountains, rivers.

Lie on grass and look at the sky. Do you see animals in the clouds?

Take a train ride.

Make a fort with blankets.

Dress up your pet.

Go to the beach and collect seashells.

Go bike riding with no destination in mind.

Make a sandcastle.

Go play in a park (swinging on the swings, etc.).

Send postcards to friends.

Make a collage.

Visit a museum.

Go to the bookstore, hang out and read in the children's book section.

Make a list of 50 things you love.

Go to an aquarium.

Visit an amusement park.

Go to a petting zoo.

Buy balloons and try to make balloon animals.

Write a story about your pet.

Compliment strangers.

Make a lemonade stand.

Go ice-skating.

Go roller-skating.

Play solitaire and see if you can beat your best score.

Take a pottery class.

Sing in the shower.

Take a dance class.

Sing into your hairbrush and dance around the living room.

Buy "lucky socks."

Drink a chocolate malt.

Wear a fake tattoo.

Make jello.

Dress up for no reason.

List 100 people you love.

Read a joke book.

Put glow in the dark stars on your bedroom ceiling.

Write a letter to Santa Claus.

Buy and complete a puzzle.

Watch *The Wizard of Oz*.

Dress up like a rock star.

Write a love letter to yourself.

Visit a sacred space.

Make a card for someone you love.

Write a thank you note to your imaginary friend.

Speak in rhyme or pig-Latin.

Paint with watercolors.

Make hand shadows.

Make a sock puppet and create a character.

Buy a goldfish.

Make a mask.

Dress like you're going to a masquerade ball.

Make a book of quotes from your friends.

Look at your old photo albums.

Go to a toy store and explore.

Buy a squirt gun and squirt things on a walk.

Go fly a kite.

Collect beautiful leaves.

Bake homemade cookies.

Scan the QR code for bonus materials and video trainings:

9

Reclaiming Your Personal Power

"Our deepest fear is not that we are inadequate. Our deepest fear is that we are powerful beyond measure. It is our light, not our darkness that most frightens us."

—Marianne Williamson

Anna had a first date with a guy who lived a few hours from her. After communicating through a dating app and on the phone, he decided to take the train to her city so they could spend the weekend together. Meeting him at the station, Anna was a bit disappointed that the chemistry she'd imagined between them wasn't present at all. They started their weekend at a café, and their conversation quickly became awkward. Not wanting him to feel disappointed about the trip, she suggested they go to a museum down the street. This occurred again and again; their interactions wouldn't go well, and Anna would suggest another activity or a different location, hoping that somehow their disconnection would transform into compatibility. She was playing tour guide for a man she barely knew.

We like to be efficient in our coaching sessions and not get bogged down with plot details, with that goal we often ask our clients to avoid giving us the play-by-play of individual dating experiences. Instead, we ask them to jump right to sharing their feelings about the events. Anna had been coaching with us regularly and had become accustomed to this instruction, but this time when we asked her to skip straight to her feelings, she uncharacteristically raised her voice and demanded she tell us every detail. We obliged, and as she plodded along giving us all the specifics, something interesting occurred—she interrupted herself, and her voice filled with emotion as she very sweetly apologized for having yelled at us. She shared this powerful insight: "I just realized that I wanted to tell you every single thing that happened because I needed you both to tell me that my behavior was acceptable." This breakthrough after Anna's emotional breakdown was the tipping point, her moment of realization that she is her own authority. After this session, her confidence grew, and she took charge of her dating life; instead of trying to fix awkward situations, she began to embrace having uncomfortable conversations and making requests. The man she eventually married willingly made changes for her because her happiness mattered to him. In our coaching, we provide tools (rather than rules) as well as guardrails, and we function as guides to love. This way each client can become their own authority and reclaim their personal power.

Reclaiming your personal power means that you trust yourself on your journey to love; you're no longer letting Your Love Imprint drag you into unhealthy and unsatisfying relationships. You're able to recognize and disengage from your emotional stories. You don't look to others or to society for approval, and you make decisions by trusting your emotional life, your gut, and your intuition to govern your choices. You're no longer sacrificing yourself or your needs as an

> *Reclaiming your personal power means that you trust yourself on your journey to love; you're no longer letting Your Love Imprint drag you into unhealthy and unsatisfying relationships.*

attempt to earn love, and you accept that being human comes with having flaws. No longer in reaction to the past, you're beginning to see a vision of love that's expansive and supports you on the path to your highest and best self. Your new mantra is, "I am my own authority!"

Reclaiming Authority of Your Emotional Life

After giving a speech at a women's group, an acquaintance of Orna's said to her, "Oh, I know I can't trust my feelings. Emotions don't last, like you said, so I don't give them any importance." This woman reached out to us after she'd been dating a guy she really liked for a few months. "I just realized all my stuff is coming up and I don't want to mess this up," she confessed.

Discounting, ignoring, or justifying your emotions will never serve you, because your feelings are data, informing you about your state of being. When you learn to trust your emotions and listen to what they're trying to tell you, you start to welcome them and use them as a guide. Your emotions are signals from your subconscious attempting to communicate something important to you, but your subconscious doesn't communicate directly in English (or French, or Swahili, or whatever your native language is). It communicates through your body as physical sensations, and the body can be seen as a metaphor that helps bring clarity to your feeling state.

The metaphors commonly used, like "shouldering responsibility," "butterflies in my stomach," or "it felt like a punch to the gut," indicate not only the location in the body but also what a particular emotion is trying to communicate. These metaphors reveal a tremendous amount of information about your state of being and profound insights regarding your emotional experiences beyond simply feeling sad, angry, or hurt. You could imagine that your subconscious mind lives in your physical body, and where your emotions manifest in the body gives you information about the underlying issue. Tuning into your body and examining where your feelings reside helps bring you into rapport with your subconscious mind and guides you to break the patterns of your emotional stories.

Tuning into your body and examining where your feelings reside guides you to break the patterns of your emotional stories.

Mental and emotional stress manifest in the body as physical symptoms. When you're out of rapport with yourself, it can manifest as disease in the body. In her groundbreaking work *The Molecules of Emotion*, neuroscientist Candace Pert revealed how the mind–body connection functions through the chemistry of the brain and that all emotion is chemical. When you experience an emotion, these chemicals are released into the organs and tissues of the body. If the emotion is not expressed or processed, the chemical will stay in the organs and tissues and produce an imbalance in the body. Getting into rapport with your emotional life will not only improve your overall mental health, it will also strengthen your immune system and keep your body healthy and functioning.

The subconscious metaphors of your emotional life are best understood by examining the parts of your body, the issues inherent in those body parts, and the common emotions associated with them. You'll discover how each of the six core negative emotions—fear, anger, sadness, hurt, shame, and guilt—manifests in each area. And using the wisdom of the ancient yogis and the chakra system, you'll discover how these energy centers that run from the base of your spine to the top of your head play a role in revealing the source of your emotional distress. The seven major chakras—crown, third eye, throat, heart, solar plexus, sacral, and root, are tied to nerve bundles and internal organs. Keep in mind that we're not referencing the chakra centers as part of a path to spiritual enlightenment (that's a whole different book); instead, we're roughly utilizing the chakra system, combined with other parts of the body, to discuss that where your emotions manifest reveals more insight into your emotional state.

Starting at the top of the head, the crown chakra represents your spiritual self and your overall well-being. Sadness and hurt stemming from isolation typically collect in this area as the crown chakra is related to your connection to source, the universe, something larger than yourself.

Next, we come to the third eye chakra, located just above the space between your eyebrows, which is the center of your vision, intuition, and ability to make decisions. Fear is commonly found here, particularly the fear of making the wrong decision. Headaches can often stem from the stress of struggling with indecision.

Your eyes represent your ability to see clearly. Sadness welling up in the eyes, often in the form of tears, can cloud your ability to see the truth or can come from not liking what you see in your life.

Your jaw and mouth represent your ability to express yourself. Clenching your jaw can indicate biting back your words or being unable to speak up; this region is associated with anger and fear.

Your throat chakra, located at your throat, is your communication center and the ability to speak your truth. Fear, guilt, and shame are commonly found here, as in the fear of speaking your truth or the shame of not being able to speak up for yourself.

The back of your neck and upper shoulders can indicate taking too much responsibility or not taking on your share; you may experience guilt or anger here. This can be felt through tension or pain in your neck and shoulders.

The center of your chest below your throat is your heart chakra. It is your emotional center and the source of love and joy. Negative emotions commonly felt here are hurt and sadness. These feelings can also be present in your anatomical heart, as opposed to the center of your chest.

Your solar plexus chakra (the area a few fingers above the belly button to just under your sternum), is connected to your inner power and self-confidence. Anger, fear, and guilt are often associated with this part of the body.

Your stomach and gut are where you process and digest your food and represent your ability to process your feelings. Common feelings felt here are fear, guilt, and shame.

Your spine and lower back are connected to feeling supported in your life, with your mid-back connected to emotional support and your lower back connected to financial support. Emotions felt here include hurt, anger, and fear.

Your sacral chakra, at your pelvis, is the source of your creativity and sexuality. Feelings of guilt or shame can be present here, particularly guilt about your sexuality, or shame about sexual desires and experiences.

Your root chakra, at the base of your pelvis, is related to your safety and security; it's common for fear to stem from this area.

Your arms and hands are the fight part of the fight/flight response and therefore connected to anger. Your legs and feet are the flight response and are associated with fear.

Paying attention to where you experience emotions as well as the sensations present allows you to disengage from the emotional story you've tied to a particular emotional state. Instead of fretting about why you keep meeting the same kind of emotionally unavailable person, you can explore the sadness that feels like a pit in your stomach. For example, a sad, heavy sensation in your gut reveals that you've self-abandoned by looking for love and approval from someone who's incapable of giving it to you. Reclaiming your personal power occurs when you take ownership of your lovability instead of putting it in someone else's hands.

Maya tended to lose herself in her relationships; she would set aside her wants and needs, constantly apologizing and downplaying her emotions until she couldn't take it anymore and eventually exploded, ending the relationship. This strategy was a manifestation of her love imprint, "I don't count or matter in love." Since she believed that she didn't count or matter, she didn't trust herself to select an ideal partner, and she felt powerless through the dating process. Either she felt vulnerable and helpless or guarded and closed off. She was so disconnected from her feelings she struggled to differentiate them from her thoughts. Every time we asked her to pinpoint where she felt guilt, anger, or sadness in her body, they all originated from her upper stomach, just below the sternum. It made sense that her issues with personal power showed up in her solar plexus, the source of power in the body. Believing that she didn't count or matter had left her feeling powerless in her relationships. Giving herself permission to experience negative emotions and the SHYFT to express them allowed her to stop ignoring and suppressing her desires, emotions, and intelligence and to assert her power. The shift that occurred was feeling more grounded in her body and more confident as she moved through the world as well as in the dating process.

Once she felt centered and no longer caught in the pendulum swing of feeling powerless, she refused to take back the on-again, off-again relationship she always knew would go nowhere. Finally free of the cycle of taking him back again and again at his whim, she took time to heal her heart and grow her self-confidence by stretching outside of her comfort zone in every area of her life. Maya changed her job, moved across the country, and started her life over.

After settling in her city and new job, she started dating again, this time with intention and purpose. All of her practice with the SHYFT communication allowed her to experience that she did count and matter because her feelings mattered. She began to quickly deselect wishy-washy, noncommittal guys without all the anguish and deliberations of the past. Soon she met a man who stepped up and let her know his intentions from the start. Maya is still a bit surprised that claiming her personal power was the secret to finding the love of her life.

Examining where your emotions are located in the body (particularly any pattern you can identify) assists you with emotional mastery as well as reclaiming your power. The goal is to separate the emotional story from the sensations and emotions that are stuck energy in that correlating part of the body. Coming from curiosity—rather than indulging the story in your head, or the search for *why* you have an emotional pattern again or got triggered again—leads to a new perspective of your emotional reactions, putting you in the driver's seat to make adjustments so you can shift your response.

When you're focused on *why* you're having an emotional reaction, you're still caught up in the story of the emotion. Instead, when you focus on the physical metaphor of the emotion, you can get to the root of the issue without getting caught up in the story. For example, "I'm feeling angry that you keep interrupting me and that's just like my father would do, telling me I'm stupid." Versus, "I'm feeling anger and tightness in my throat. This anger is connected to my emotional story that I don't have a right to express myself." Notice how the second version gives you something to work with to reconnect to your power. You can't change the circumstances of your past, and focusing on the circumstances keeps you stuck in the past. However, you can change the meaning you give to those events and reclaim your power.

Different emotions have different levels of energy and vibrate at different frequencies. For example, depression tends to drain all the energy out of you, while anger energizes and motivates you to take action. Imagine that your emotions are different levels of energetic vibrations, like they're located at different spots along a totem pole. At the top, the emotion with the highest vibrational energy is bliss. At the bottom, like the stump of the totem pole in the ground, is shame. Shame holds the lowest energy of all emotions because shame is attached to your identity and instigates feelings of being broken, bad, and wrong. Near the top of the totem pole is authenticity; it holds a very high vibrational energy. Many people are afraid of feeling or expressing their anger, but anger has energy in it; without anger you may not be motivated to make changes. We had a meeting with a consultant who said, "I bet you don't like working with angry clients. That would be exhausting." We answered, "We love working with clients who are angry about not having a loving life partner (or angry at an ex) because they're motivated to take action to change their circumstances."

Your emotional energy is contagious, and it easily spreads from one person to another like glitter. When you're mindful of your own emotional energy, you can retreat from others when you're having a bad day and make a point of being social when you're feeling good. Remember, there's no cherry-picking your emotions; as a human being you're here to feel the full range of emotions— they're just temporary. Having a healthy relationship with your emotional life helps build your resilience when situations go awry. When events don't go your way, practice bouncing back from an upset as quickly as possible. See if you can create a new habit of getting into a new resourceful state rather than a negative downward spiral. That doesn't mean you want to rush through negative emotions; instead, acknowledge and experience them fully, so you can move on and not let them pile up.

Reclaiming Authority over Your Decisions

Carol struggled with the fear of choosing the wrong man. Feeling left behind because her friends were all married and starting families, Carol felt adrift in her dating life. She was raised in a traditional Catholic family and embraced her faith but felt constrained by her community's expectations of a traditional family. She desperately wanted children, and she loved her career. Her fear of making the wrong choice in love caused her to spend way too much time with men who weren't a good match but were part of her religious community, and therefore she gave them a lot more leeway than most.

Carol's love imprint, "I'm a disappointment in love," created an internal struggle between what she imagined was expected of her versus her true desires. Having come from a very close loving family, she felt like she was a disappointment. Now that all her friends were married, she was the last one unwed and stone-cold single. She was so stuck in her head that she felt frozen—wanting to get married and afraid she was letting down everyone she cared about. We taught Carol to trust her emotional guidance system and gave her tools for making decisions so she would stop ruminating over every choice in her life. Once her energy was freed up and unfrozen, she stopped looking for any guy and focused on finding the right match for her long-term. She quickly met a man who was in alignment with her religious and spiritual upbringing who she also found incredibly attractive. After spending a year dating and integrating their friendship pool, they got engaged and then married the following year. She got her dream come true that her kids would be playing with her best friends' kids, because they are now expecting baby number two.

Fear of making the wrong decision, particularly the wrong decision in love, is so incredibly common that you're going to learn how to bust this forevermore and never struggle to make a choice. These methods help you make important decisions with both your head and heart in harmony creating a life filled with more joy and fulfillment. If you struggle to make decisions, embracing these practices will add time and cultivate inner peace in every part of your life.

We teach two different strategies for making decisions. The first tool is to flip a coin. It may appear frivolous on the surface, but it's a surefire way to make decisions quickly, especially if you struggle making a choice or have difficulty deciding what you really want. This tool is best used for quick decisions, like what to eat at a restaurant or which movie you want to watch. Sometimes in life it's important to act quickly and make a choice so that opportunities don't pass you by. For the coin option, first assign one option to the "heads" side and one to the "tails" side before you flip it. The fun part is getting to know yourself through your heart and not your brain. If you're standing at the taco stand and you're not sure whether to order steak or chicken, flip a coin. You aren't using the coin to make the decision for you; you're using the coin to reveal which choice you truly desire. Upon seeing which side the coin lands, you'll immediately be either disappointed or pleased; either way, you'll know what to order. Do this often, and you'll get in the habit of deciding quickly and easily.

The second decision-making tool is designed to help you make weighty decisions without creating an elaborate list of pros and cons and leaving your heart out of it. Implement this for more important decisions where you feel you're at a crossroads and unsure of which way to turn. These can be two options that really pull at you and you're just not sure which way to go. When you have a choice about a life path, your logical brain is limited with only binary choices of right or wrong, but most of your big life decisions aren't so black and white.

Let's go through this exercise together. Select two activities you enjoy. We'd pick two activities we both love to indulge in. For the sake of this exercise, let's call them Option A, going to Disneyland, and Option B, going sailing. Sitting down with your legs uncrossed and your feet flat on the floor, place the palms of your hands on your thighs. Feel your feet on the floor and the weight and warmth of your hands on your thighs. Ground yourself in your body and come into the present moment by becoming aware of your sensory experience. Feel your hips in the chair, feel the temperature in the room. Look for different colors; maybe you see the colors green, brown, or red. Become aware of the light source in the room. Take a few deep breaths, releasing the stress of the day.

Next, picture your Option A in your mind's eye (you can do this with your eyes open or closed, whichever works best for you). Using our example, we would imagine riding the rides, the immersive adventures, and having dinner at Downtown Disney—the whole theme park experience. Consider how you'll feel during and after the imagined day with your Option A. Now come back to the present moment by grounding again. From a clear mind, picture your Option B. Imagine the other people you're with, if applicable, and the fun you'll have. Be sure to include how you'll feel during and after the activity with all the details you can be sure of. We'd picture starting at the marina, boarding the boat, and spending the day on the water. Now drop into your heart, place your hands on your heart center one on top of the other, take a deep breath, and ask yourself this important question, "Which do I want to experience?" Your heart will reveal the answer to you. Ultimately, the decision-making process is choosing the *experience* you prefer, not the destination (and not about right or wrong).

When you're using this tool for future decisions, you can use it for anything: deciding between two jobs, or two houses to purchase, or two cities to live in. Picture your future at Option A and then at Option B. Zero in on the feelings of each experience and ask your heart which encounter you favor.

In *The Wizard of Oz*, Dorothy leaves Munchkin Land with only one directive: "Follow the yellow brick road." Not too far into her journey she comes to an intersection and she's not sure which way will take her to the Emerald City. Behind her is Munchkin Land, but she has no idea if she should continue straight or turn right or left. Then she meets the Scarecrow, and at the end of the song they head off in a direction. They make a choice and find their way to the Emerald City. We wholeheartedly believe if they had gone in either of the other two directions they still would have ended up at the Emerald City, but they wouldn't have met the Cowardly Lion or the Tin Man. They would have had different experiences, perhaps meeting a shy purple penguin and a frightened polka-dotted llama. The question to ask yourself when making a decision is to discover which *experience* you prefer.

Using Fear as a Guide

Imagine yourself at your highest and best self. What do you look like? How is your hair styled? What are you wearing? What's the expression on your face? Where do you think you'd be living? No matter the details you try to dream up, you can't get a completely clear picture because your highest and best self exists in your blind spot. This version of you is not visible to you, but you can find the path to get there because there's a forcefield of fear around it. The journey to your soulmate is a journey of personal growth, a journey of becoming the best version of yourself. That path isn't always clear at first, but there's an energy around it that you'll experience as fear (because it's unknown). We've shared how to make fear your friend in Chapter Five, but now let's take that concept further and show you how fear can guide you to the best version of yourself.

When you take actions despite having an emotional fear (without physical danger), you'll be rewarded by moving closer to your highest and best self. If you're holding on to a lot of fear and uncertainty, we ask that you play full out by running the experiment with the "Three Doors" Exercise. Healing occurs at the speed of safety, so you don't need to take any unnecessary risks. The actions we're asking you to take have zero physical danger—you won't even break a nail. Learning not to believe everything you think will serve you through this process. You've been conditioned a particular way, and in time you'll find that stepping outside your comfort zone is easy. As always, be kind, compassionate, and loving with yourself through this process.

On a blank sheet of paper, draw three doors. Label the first door "Cold," the second "Warm," and the last "Hot." Each door represents actions you take frequently or actions you avoid taking because of discomfort and fear. Cold door actions are things you often do with no fear at all. All human beings are creatures of habit, so it'll be easy for you to list these. But there's no need to write them down; instead, just take a moment and think of everything you often do with no fear at all—their outcomes are known to you, and that's why this door is "cold." Walking through this door is familiar and comfortable.

Warm door actions are just outside of your comfort zone. Think of actions you could take to improve your love life that are marginally uncomfortable for you. Make a list of any actions or tools we've shared thus far that challenge you and feel moderately uncomfortable. Maybe it's speaking up for yourself and using the SHYFT with someone you haven't yet. Perhaps it's stretching to the next step on your journey through the Steps to Emotional Authenticity. Or maybe you're putting off starting your Inner Child Dates for one reason or another. Look over your list and select three actions that give you pause, just a bit of hesitation, and write them as a list under the door marked "warm." You can also select actions you've been putting off, like asking for a raise, or asking someone for support or a favor. The actions on these two lists do not need to only come from this book.

Hot door actions are ones that feel scary and bring up a considerable amount of fear when you think about taking these actions. Make a list of the tools and actions that bring up a high level of emotional fear (remember, nothing that could cause physical harm). Now choose three of them to list under the hot door. Maybe it's joining a dating app, going on a first date, using the SHYFT to make a request, collecting your belongings from an ex, or asking an ex to settle up on the money they owe you.

Now that you've created your list of three warm door actions and three hot door actions, pull out your calendar and commit to a date you'll take all three of your warm door actions and put them all on your to-do list or on your calendar to schedule getting them done. You have a choice to add a date you'll complete all your hot door actions by as well, or you can wait until you've completed one or two of the warm door actions before assigning a date to the hot door actions. You'll discover that once you've completed a set of warm door actions, the hot door actions don't feel so scary, and you may even move some to the warm door list. The more you extend outside your comfort zone, the more you'll develop self-confidence. This can be a life-changing exercise because the more you lean into the actions that have emotional fears attached to them the more you'll become the best version of yourself. The rewards of moving outside your comfort zone make your dream life a reality. You cannot anticipate which actions will bring you a specific result, but we do encourage you to run the experiment and reap the massive rewards. Work at your own pace. The more you accomplish with regularity the better. If you don't commit to taking these actions within one to two weeks of each other, you won't gain momentum, a crucial component for becoming comfortable taking uncomfortable actions. A permanent transformation occurs over a condensed period of time, so you'll want to be mindful of the timeframe you allot for scheduling these actions.

Challenge yourself to frequently utilize this Three Doors Exercise, setting up new activities to extend beyond your comfort zone. You'll find that as you grow and move toward your highest and best self, the actions that used to be warm are now cold, and the hot actions are becoming warm. If you have a lot of resistance to getting started or being consistent with this exercise, look at yourself in the mirror and remind yourself that you are loved and safe, and that these actions aren't dangerous. Each time you move through the forcefield of fear you'll be rewarded. The tricky part is that you don't have any control over what the prize will be. Trust that you'll be better off, and if you need to, ask your higher power for support. One of the huge benefits of this Three Door Exercise is that you'll be able to identify the difference between something dangerous (that has physical danger involved) versus an emotional fear that's fictional. You've mastered this tool when you think about doing something that scares you and the first thought in your head is, "Oh crap, now I have to do that!"

In the 1990s, Orna spent an entire year facing her fears, and looking back it was a defining year that changed her life in immeasurable ways. She gave a friend his insulin shot despite her fear of needles. She went to the shooting range with a seasoned armorer on film sets and shot a gun for the first time. She completed her first triathlon (swim, bike, run event). She quit a job she'd had for over four years and moved out of state. She performed six full minutes of stand-up comedy at the world-famous Improv alongside professional comics. As Orna consistently faced her fears, her people-pleasing strategies subsided, new opportunities came her way, previously closed doors opened, and she embraced her powerful, authentic self. At the time, she had no idea that taking these actions would set the stage for her love life to remarkably change for the better.

In 2009, we had initially started Creating Love on Purpose as an in-person workshop and quickly moved everything online (which was very cutting-edge back then). Five years later, we returned to live seminars with our Getting It Right This Time® Live event. After putting down a huge deposit for a location and a production team, ticket sales were going very slowly. Three weeks out from the start, Orna panicked and told Matthew, "We can still cancel with small fees to the venue and production company, let's refund the few tickets we've sold and regroup for another time." Matthew looked Orna in the eye with a sweet smile on his face he said, "We don't *not* do things because they're scary." He may have even winked. We continue to challenge ourselves to grow toward our highest and best selves. This allows us to be of service to you in the best way possible when you need our support. We'll never ask you to commit to something we haven't done ourselves; we still practice the very same skills and tools we're sharing with you now.

Lindsay's Journey of Reclaiming Her Power

Raised in a conservative small town in the Midwest, our client Lindsay was six years old when her dad was diagnosed with a rare heart condition. At this young age Lindsay lost all certainty of the world. For the next thirty years she spent many nights in hospitals on pins and needles alongside her mother and older brother as they waited for doctors to tell them their fate. This impending doom enveloped the family with an underlying tension of chaos and uncertainty.

Lindsay's family certainly had their dysfunction; however, there was no toxic or abusive behavior, nor mental illness. She was an intelligent, sensitive girl who strived to do the right thing and never disappoint the people she loved. She worked hard at school and all of her extracurricular activities, and she prided herself on never giving up on a goal. These qualities in Lindsay's character combined with the underlying feeling of uncertainty and chaos from her dad's emergency hospital stays made her a prime fit for a particular type of toxic male who was controlling, manipulative, and narcissistic. Her marriage to the first version of this type of man lasted ten years and ended when she was thirty-one. At thirty-nine, she ended her engagement to another controlling narcissist and reached out to us upon the recognition of her pattern.

A fear of abandonment was at the root of Lindsay's troubles with men. Her relationship history created the false belief that she was bad at love and dating. In reality, Lindsay simply made choices that felt familiar to the little girl inside of her. She took on some of her mother's strategies, like being sensitive to the opinions of others. (Limiting beliefs are commonly passed down from one generation to the next.) Invested in other people's opinion of her, Lindsay believed she had to win a person's approval to be loved. Her underlying feelings of uncertainty about the future were mirrored back to her through her ex-husband's erratic moods and demands. Despite his toxic behavior, Lindsey spent years trying to make the marriage work. She was constantly being gaslit that all their problems were hers alone, and she jumped through hoop after hoop attempting to please her ex-husband and win his love and approval. Recognizing the same dynamic with her fiancé was the aha moment that prompted her to get professional help.

Our work with Lindsay began by releasing the demoralizing shame she felt for initiating the end of two significant relationships. We unraveled her attachment to winning approval, allowing her to accept her own value and grow her self-worth. Lindsay began to feel safe in her own body and in the world, as well as to trust her own feelings and desires. She had been raised to downplay her feelings, to "Get over it" and persevere, no matter what—generally, an admirable quality in the workforce, but when it comes to love relationships, this set Lindsay up to tolerate unacceptable behavior.

Lindsay's confidence in her career began to transfer over into her dating life. She could recognize potentially controlling men and move on from them quickly. As Lindsay embraced our dating strategies, one man, Jonathon, kept showing up for her in a very different way than all of her current prospects and past relationships. Her exes were always critical of her career and demanded she spend more time with them, but Jonathon would go out of his way to support her ambitions. He supported her career, including all the time she spent away from home traveling for work. She noticed a new feeling of calm in his presence and began to trust it and open her heart. Eventually, Jonathon and Lindsay committed to an exclusive relationship, and a year later they were married. Lindsay's journey to long-lasting love was intertwined with embracing her personal power rather than abdicating it. She had learned where to draw the boundary to avoid going into sacrifice, no longer making choices that fostered anger and resentment.

Lindsay describes the difference in her relationship with Jonathan from her previous partners as a calm and ease in just being herself. She's no longer walking on eggshells waiting for the other shoe to drop. She doesn't avoid conflict and is able to express her feelings without anxiously awaiting a response. With Jonathan, Lindsay can have an open and authentic dialog even when it comes to coparenting his daughter. They work through their differences from a place of love and acceptance.

Ultimately, reclaiming your personal power is up to you. It means you'll never put your lovability or acceptability in the hands of a stranger on a date. Nor will you seek approval for your feelings or behaviors from anyone other than yourself—that's real inner power! Sadly, you've been giving your power away due to the emotional stories that are tied to your past experiences in

> *Ultimately, reclaiming your personal power is up to you. It means you'll never put your lovability or acceptability in the hands of a stranger on a date.*

love, which all stem from Your Love Imprint. To create healthy, long-lasting love, you must reclaim your personal power. Your free will is always available to you. Most people walk around like zombies tied to their behavioral habits and responses as if they have no other option and allow their past experiences to define them. Your past in love doesn't have to look like your future in love because you're the one in control of your love life. Once you reclaim your personal power, you'll never be the same. You'll stop feeling like a victim and you'll start appreciating all the events that have led you to this moment in time.

Breaking the pattern of Your Love Imprint requires that you utilize the powerful tools we've given you thus far. Identifying your feelings is the foundation we started off with by setting alarms to discover your mental/emotional patterns in Chapter Two. Then, in Chapter Five the bracelet exercise brings awareness to an unconscious inner dialog that isn't supportive, and breaks the pattern of negative self-talk by replacing it with a positive affirmation. Another tool at your disposal is the laughter exercise in Chapter Five, which functions as a state break, so you can change the meaning you've assigned to past events (whether they occurred yesterday or decades ago). Working out at the authenticity gym and moving through the Steps to Emotional Authenticity from Chapter Six is a lifelong practice, along with the Speak How You Feel Template (the SHYFT). Remember the Responsibility Equation from Chapter Six so you only claim accountability for your thoughts, feelings, and actions (and no one else's). This allows you to set and maintain healthy boundaries which foster respectful love. Managing your mindset is a skill that pays off in every area of your life, including all your relationships from your children to your boss and everyone in between. Finding gratitude in heartbreak and disappointment with the golden nugget exercise from Chapter Seven allows you to find forgiveness and free yourself from energetic bonds of past hurts. Learning to serve yourself first by filling your own cup (not just to full but to overflowing so you can be of service from the overflow) ensures you won't go into sacrifice. Last, but certainly not least, is your weekly ritual of an Inner Child Date from Chapter Eight so you can reparent yourself and create a lasting bond with the child inside of you so they don't meddle with your selection of a life partner or sabotage your relationships.

The tools and exercises we've given you thus far are like different instruments that make up an orchestra. Some of them may come easily for you, and others might be more challenging. Now is the time to start utilizing these tools as if they're different sections and instruments in an orchestra and create harmony in every part of your life.

LOVE ON PURPOSE EXERCISE—REWRITE YOUR LOVE LIFE

You have a choice about the meaning you assign to the events of your life. You can choose to see yourself as a victim of circumstance and abdicate your personal power to outside forces, or you can choose to focus on everything positive that's happened through the course of your life. What you focus on grows, so choose wisely.

On one sheet of paper (not a digital device), write out two versions of your life story:

1. **Version One:** Everything bad that happened to you, including all your disappointments and failures. This is your victim story that leaves you feeling powerless and at the mercy of events.

2. **Version Two:** Everything positive that happened, all your accomplishments and achievements, everything you've learned through your challenges, how you've become a better person over time. You can use your lifetime achievement journal as a guide.

Read version one out loud to yourself and notice how it makes you feel when you focus on the negative. Put it aside and read version two and notice how it makes you feel when you focus on the positive.

You get to decide which version is the story of your life. You're the one who chooses how to define yourself and your future; no one else can. Pick one version to keep and refer to and burn the other one. Release the one you no longer want to hold on to and say aloud, "I release this for my highest good." If you don't have a fireplace or a safe place outdoors to have a fire, you can always burn a piece of paper in your kitchen sink. Turn on the vent above your stove to keep smoke from accumulating. Set yourself free from the negative events of the past and concentrate on the ability to be positive and create positive outcomes in your life.

Scan the QR code for bonus materials and video trainings:

PART 3

Manifestation

What Does Love Mean to You?

"Love does not consist in gazing at each other,
but in looking outward together in the same direction."
—Antoine de Saint-Exupery

Anneliese knew exactly what she didn't want in a life partner. During her marriage, she felt chronically anxious, and now that it was over, she felt frustrated and angry. She was annoyed that she was a single mom and angry that she was in a constant power struggle with her ex over raising their son.

Growing up, her father demanded attention and respect; he was ambitious to a fault. He demanded to be the king of the family and prided himself on showing everyone how successful he was. Her mother was the opposite; she instilled in Anneliese and her younger brother the importance of being part of the community, and that to fit in they must be modest and not draw attention to themselves by boasting or bragging. These mixed messages created a lot of insecurity and low self-worth that followed Anneliese into adulthood. As a girl she tried to win her father's attention and respect by excelling in school and showering him with praise and admiration. Due to his narcissism, it was never enough, and that's exactly how she felt inside—always lacking, never feeling like she was worthy of the love she desired.

Throughout her dating life, she would cling to men who were attentive, and she would sacrifice her own needs and desires, attempting to earn love and acceptance. She was good at adjusting to people, surroundings, and new situations, but with men she found it difficult to relax and be herself; she was riddled with anxiety. As an attractive woman she had no trouble finding men to date, but the ones she partnered with were selfish, emotionally unavailable, and did not respect her. The man she married left her without explanation a few years after their son was born. The false belief of her love imprint that she couldn't count on love was a self-filling prophecy. Most of all, she wished to rid herself of feeling apprehensive and wanted someone who would be kind and consistent so she could relax and rely on them.

Anneliese's journey to her beloved is not unique. She spent a lot of time getting in touch with her feeling state, learning to speak up for herself and making requests. She embraced the idea of teaching someone how to treat her and leaned into her fears with our encouragement. Every experience of being authentic grew her self-worth, and much to her delight, her anxiety vanished. It became clear to her that she mostly desired a partner who would treat her kindly, with respect, and support her ambitions. Today Anneliese is happily married to Peter, who showers her with attention and even encouraged her to quit her unfulfilling dead-end job and start a new business venture of her own. He's a kind and gentle man and a wonderful role model for her son as he enters adolescence. Manifestation became easy for Anneliese once she had a clear vision of her beloved relationship and how it would function. Peter was an excellent match for her because he created a safe space for her to relax, and also shared her vision of creating something larger than just the two of them. As her business grows, they have a shared goal of working together to make the world a better place.

Every person is fighting for love on their terms without consciously deciding what their terms are. At sixteen or seventeen years old, you didn't sit down and create a vision of your ideal relationship, decide what it should look like, and how it should function. Instead, your conditions for love were cobbled together by your experiences. The people you found attractive were likely a match to your core wound—Your Love Imprint. Your experiences in love were haphazard at best and traumatic at worst.

When you've been hurt and disappointed in love, it's easy to fall into the trap of repeating those painful situations. Unfortunately, there's also a strong emotional charge on the people and circumstances from those experiences. Manifestation requires you to have a clear vision imbued with powerful emotions—therefore, if you're focused on what you don't want it's very easy to recreate it over and over again. Rather than having a clear vision of what you desire in love your goal ends up being the opposite of what you don't want. But what your heart desires isn't the opposite of those painful experiences. You can't create the opposite of what you don't want because you can't manifest from lack.

Whatever you focus on grows, so trying to avoid pain from past experiences can get you caught up in a vicious cycle of repeating those unhealthy patterns you're trying to avoid. If we asked you to *not* think of a pink elephant, what would you do? First, you'd have to think of a pink elephant, and then try to negate the image in your mind. The more you tried *not* to think of a pink elephant, the more you'd be thinking of a pink elephant. By focusing on what you don't want, you're continuing to create a self-fulfilling prophecy to end up with more of what you don't want. To break the cycle, you must discover your terms for love.

A common approach to manifesting your ideal partner is to make a list of the qualities you desire in a significant other. Most people's lists read like they're ordering off a menu with comprehensive details of appearance and personality (like hair and eye color, the make and model of the car they drive, and their tax bracket). This list isn't useful in your search for lasting love because it has nothing to do with your heart's desires; it's focused on external qualities that have nothing to do with the dynamic between you. We had one client who came to us convinced her soulmate would be a pilot with a private plane. Another insisted on asking every prospect on a second date if they had any debt. Your heart couldn't care less about such things! The more detailed and specific your list, the easier it is for you to reject potential matches for superficial reasons. We beg you to toss out your list so you can date with curiosity and evaluate a match as you measure them up to the vision of your true soul partnership.

Your ideal relationship likely won't be like ours. We practically spend 24/7, 365 together because we're married partners who also work together in our business. Our relationship should be stamped, "For Professionals Only, Please Don't Try This at Home." Not all married couples should work together. Some very happy and healthy couples don't even live in the same house. Your ideal relationship can look however you like, and you'll want to create that vision now, *before* you commit and go exclusive.

Your terms for love are the qualities that you value in your intimate relationship. They're the promise of what can be when you create your ideal relationship on your terms. If your terms for love are solely in response to past hurts and frustrations, then you're going to be stuck in a negative pattern, finding what you don't want over and over again because avoiding pain isn't a strategy for creating a healthy relationship. (Remember, what you want isn't the opposite of what you don't want.)

Your terms for love are the qualities that you value in your intimate relationship. They're the promise of what can be when you create your ideal relationship on your terms.

What are you willing to fight for? What are your needs that you can never sacrifice? It's important to make a distinction between your needs and wants. Your needs are *not* negotiable, but your wants are. Knowing the difference between your needs and your wants brings clarity to your search for an ideal life partner. For you to feel loved, your partner must satisfy your needs a majority of the time. Get clear on the dynamic you desire between the two of you. How do you like to be treated when you don't feel well? When you're upset? How do you like to celebrate your birthday or other achievements? How important is family to you? Knowing your terms for love makes it easy to identify an ideal match through the dating process.

When we ask our clients about their terms for love, communication is one of the most common qualities they list. Suppose they value communication because their parents didn't communicate kindly or respectfully, or their ex never communicated feelings with them, and they felt disconnected and alone. In this case, their desire for communication is emotionally entangled with avoiding the hurt, anger, or sadness from someone either not communicating (shutting them out) or doing so in an unkind manner. By desiring communication in an intimate relationship, they'll look for someone who communicates well. The problem could be that *they're* the one who doesn't communicate consistently with a partner, or they haven't mastered the skills to do it well. It's easy to communicate when they're getting along, like in the early stage of dating, but they struggle to communicate when they're upset (they'll clam up or act out). In this case, their actions are out of alignment with their desires. The unrealistic expectation that their partner will make up for their deficiencies means they're out of integrity. If you discover through this journey that you're expecting to have a partner that makes up for your own shortcomings, revisit the Ho'oponopono exercise in Chapter Seven to come back into integrity with yourself by forgiving that younger version of you and continuing to practice the tools and techniques for being authentic.

The flip side of this scenario is that if the desire for communication wasn't tied to past hurts, they would consistently be sharing their thoughts and feelings with their partner because it keeps them emotionally connected. It's interesting to note if communication was something you were good at, consistent with, and desired from a partner you'd only choose a partner who communicated well. You'd deselect a bad communicator early on because they're simply not a good match for you. You wouldn't feel angry or hurt if your date didn't communicate well; you'd deselect them and move on without another thought because they're not a values match for you. They would never live rent free in your head or your heart.

To discover your terms for love, we'd like you to exercise your imagination and think of someone who has a healthy relationship. You admire this person for their ability to keep their relationship healthy, happy, and thriving. It can be someone you know, a public figure, or someone famous that you respect. It could even be a character in a book, movie, or a play. Once you've chosen the person, imagine what makes them tick in their love life. If you could get inside their head and their heart, what are their terms for love? What do you imagine are their values that make them a great life partner?

As an example, let's use Tom Hanks, the actor. He and his wife Rita Wilson have been happily married for over 35 years and have spoken often of their love for each other in the press. Let's imagine dropping into Tom's heart to determine what he most values in their relationship. It's apparent he values respect and communication. His belief that lasting love doesn't happen by accident reflects his values of growth, intimacy, and connection. Actions he takes make it evident he values love and passion. Considering your avatar's terms for love allows you to list the qualities of their relationship that you believe motivates them. Now you can create your own terms for love using your avatar's list as a template to get started.

Your terms for love are about the dynamic between you and your partner. Maybe you value trust or kindness, adventure or passion, growth or support. Imagine how your ideal relationship would function and the values that are important to you in an intimate relationship. In our relationship, we both place a high value on connection. When there's a conflict or disagreement between us, it feels uncomfortable that we're no longer energetically connected. We're always motivated to address our disagreements and resolve them quickly. There are no cold wars in our home; we don't let issues fester. Instead, we clean up our differences as they emerge. Our relationship isn't perfect, but because we're both motivated to create connection, we have the uncomfortable conversations and work through our differences to get back on the same page.

Having important conversations with someone you're dating is a great way to discover who they are and whether you're compatible; however, you can't find out what someone values simply by asking them. Values are revealed over time. For example, no one is going to admit they don't value honesty or family;

You can't find out what someone values simply by asking them. Values are revealed over time.

they're not going to say, "Of course, I don't value honesty. I just lied to you five minutes ago." Questioning someone about how they may or may not respond in a hypothetical situation isn't going to reveal what you need to know either. Most people don't have the self-reflection to be reliable even if they're not trying to be manipulative, so it's unlikely you're getting an accurate assessment. The only way to discover a person's values is by spending quality time with them over a period of time and evaluating how they spend their resources: time, energy, and money. The person who's washing and waxing their car every weekend values their automobile. The person who spends every Thursday going to their parents' house for dinner values their family. Paying attention to how and where someone spends their resources will inform you of their values.

For Jessie, family was essential. Most of her weekends were spent with her parents and sisters as they were very close and supportive and helped raise Jessie's daughter. When she met Domingo, she felt she had someone who shared her values, and she thought he was a good match. He told her many times that family was very important to him. After dating for several months, Jessie hadn't yet met Domingo's family, and she was spending less time with hers because he wanted her all to himself when they were together. The shock that brought Jessie into coaching with us was the discovery that she was the other woman. Domingo had been taking his other girlfriend to family events. Jessie realized she'd abandoned one of her most important values to be with him. It tormented her that she'd given up treasured time with her family to see him. She felt like she had betrayed herself, and on some level she had. Our work together started with Jessie forgiving herself for having sacrificed her values in order to be accommodating. When she allowed herself to feel all the icky feelings of the betrayal, she could forgive herself and start dating again. This time she knew to pay attention to a guy's actions and not just listen to his words. Most importantly, Jessie learned a powerful lesson of not being too accommodating in order to win love, approval, or acceptance.

It's likely you won't be an exact values match with anyone; a majority match is all you need for an ideal relationship. Just like life throws you curveballs as a single person, the same will occur when you're partnered up. When you're in a relationship with someone who values the same things as you, you're able to get back on the same page when there's conflict. Combining shared values with chemistry, compatible lifestyles, and communication is the recipe for longevity in a loving partnership. Chemistry comes from your energetic differences. Lifestyle compatibility is important so that you have enough in common to want to spend time together. Shared values are the glue that holds the relationship together. And communication allows you to reconnect and repair when there's a disagreement. The specifics of your desired lifestyle and why those things are important to you—what you value—are your terms for love.

Combining shared values with chemistry, compatible lifestyles, and communication is the recipe for longevity in a loving partnership.

Along with knowing your terms for love, it's imperative that you embrace slow love. This means you'll allow dating to be a process, taking time to get to know someone before committing your heart or your body. Slow love includes delaying exclusivity until you're certain the two of you want the same things from a relationship. If you're dating casually and aren't interested in finding a life partner, then these concepts don't apply to you. However, when you're dating for a soulmate, slow love is the recipe for using discernment to select an ideal person for the long term. It's also the key to breaking the pattern of Your Love Imprint, which has your mind highlighting the person who is a match to your core wound.

Rushing into exclusivity or physical intimacy is not going to get you the long-lasting love you desire and deserve. Slow love is an important strategy to embrace and master because it's the only way to avoid the trap of another love imprint match. Your Love Imprint has been guiding your choices in love for your entire life, and it will take some time for you to course correct and find the path to your soulmate. It takes time to know if you can move through conflict together and if you two share the same values. Your terms for love are what you're willing to fight for and never sacrifice, and it may take you some time in the dating process to cultivate discernment and discover your values. It may appear to be counterintuitive, but practicing slow love speeds up the process of finding your ideal match.

Practicing slow love speeds up the process of finding your ideal match.

For one thing, you'll stop having short-term relationships that don't pan out and require you to heal your heart and get back out in the dating pool again and again. Slow love can shave years off your search for an ideal long-term match. There's no need to rush, because when you've met your forever person, you'll have the rest of your lives to spend together. If your goal is to share your life with the love of your life, to be with someone who values you, gets you, and will stick by you no matter what, you must practice slow love through the dating process.

Your Vision for Love

We've taken you on a journey to clear your relationship baggage and free yourself from past conditioning. Now you're prepared to begin the process of manifestation. Many dating programs start here because this is the fun part—creating the vision of your ideal relationship. However, it doesn't make sense to create your vision until you've cleaned up the muck that's been clouding your ability to clearly identify and describe your heart's desires. Please do not skip this section thinking you already know what you want, or you've done this before. You're no longer the same person who started reading at Chapter One; you have a new toolbox and skills to practice. Plus, once you're no longer afraid of re-creating past patterns or choosing the wrong person; you're ready to imagine your life alongside your soulmate. The clarity you've gained about yourself, your patterns, and your terms for love lays the groundwork for manifesting your true soul partnership.

To create the love you want, you must be able to see it. People often say, "I can't see myself doing that," and when they do, they're speaking a literal truth—they can't create a picture in their mind of taking that particular action. Whether it's speaking on stage in front of 3,000 people or jumping out of an airplane, if you can't create an image in your mind of taking that action, it feels impossible or improbable that you'll ever do it. However, if you can see yourself taking a particular action, then it feels possible or probable that you can and will do it. It's simply a matter of deciding you want to do it and taking the actions necessary to make it happen. Think of something you've never done that's unlikely you'll ever do—like climbing Mt. Everest or giving a speech in front of the United Nations. Now, try to imagine yourself in that activity. It's likely you can't create a clear picture of you doing it. However, if you were able to see yourself climbing Mt. Everest or giving a speech in front of the United Nations, then it wouldn't feel so impossible for you to achieve that goal. There'd be many steps along the way that you may or may not be willing to take, but you'd know if you committed yourself that you could achieve it. Being able to see yourself in a relationship with your true soul partner and creating a specific vision for the relationship gives you the inner belief that you can achieve your goal.

Visualization is a powerful tool, and the more specific and fleshed out your vision is the better. Ask yourself these questions: "What evidence would I need to know that I'm with my beloved? What's happening that lets me know that this is my person?" When our client Nicolette was crafting the vision of her ideal relationship, she always knew that whoever her beloved ended up being, he would be at the table for Christmas dinner in Florida. Every year since she was a little girl, her entire family rented the same three houses near the beach to get away from the biting cold of Canada for the holidays. And every year, they shared a huge feast for Christmas dinner. Nicolette knew that the man who would be sitting at that Christmas dinner in that house with her would be her soulmate. They'd be there along with all the members of her extended family, and he'd fit in as part of the group. That would be the evidence she would need to know it was her person. Not every client of ours experiences exactly what they envision through this exercise, but Nicolette was very specific about her sensory experience, so when Cyrille joined her family for Christmas dinner in Florida, she had no doubt he was the one for her. Nicolette initially came to us brokenhearted because she was dumped out of the blue by her ex; she thought she'd wasted her last opportunity to have children of her own. Now she has two with Cyrille plus stepchildren and is living her dream life with the love of her life! This is the power of visualization in action.

The vision of your soulmate relationship can include other people in it, like Nicolette's vision, or it can be just the two of you. Select a location that you already know very well. You can close your eyes and imagine what it's like to reexperience that setting. Don't choose a place you've never actually been to. If you've dreamed of going to Paris with your beloved, don't select it as a location for this exercise if you've never actually been to Paris or only passed through decades ago. It's difficult to create a clear vision of somewhere you've never been. You'll be making up too many details for your visualization to be compelling. In order to be effective, you'll need a location you've actually been to and know very well. This way your imagination has enough details to grab onto. Then, imagine an event in the future that hasn't happened yet. The more specific the better, and include all your senses—what you see, hear, touch, smell, and taste. The more details you can describe through your sensory experience, the more you're training your subconscious to guide you to your goal.

The most important thing is to decide on the evidence you'll need to know this is your person. Is it an action they take or a quality they have? Is it the location you're in, like with Nicolette? Is it the way they treat you at a specific event? For the next Love on Purpose exercise, you don't have to become the best creative writer on earth to produce your vision; just tap into the specifics of your sensory experience. Like an old-fashioned camera, your vision is either in focus or out of focus—you'll want to dial it in so it's sharp and crystal clear. This gives your subconscious new coordinates, a new directive to guide you to your soulmate.

Once you create the vision, take actions consistently to see it come to fruition. You wouldn't create a vision of you climbing Mt. Everest and then sit at home expecting you can climb the tallest mountain on earth. Creating your vision doesn't bring it to you; it steers you in the right direction and helps you avoid any obstacle that doesn't fit the vision. A common mistake with the practice of visualization is believing that creating the vision is all you need to make it happen. The truth is the vision is important for you to *believe* that you can create it, but actions are still required. There are steps you need to take to make your vision come to life. You'll discover the action steps in the next few chapters.

LOVE ON PURPOSE EXERCISES

These exercises are designed to bring clarity to the vision of your ideal relationship. Remember, having a clear vision allows you to manifest your beloved partnership.

Your Terms for Love

Write down a list of ten to twelve values that are important to you in your intimate relationship. List only the dynamic qualities between you and your soulmate, *not the qualities of a person.* See if you can create a list that inspires you. Some examples included in this chapter are communication, family, and connection. Utilize the example from this chapter and choose a person you'd like to emulate for your list of values. Zero in on qualities that inspire you as this will make the exercise much more effective. Looking over your list should excite you and create a sensation of joy and anticipation. You don't have to plug all the loopholes with your list. Focus on what inspires and motivates you.

There's no need to include the appearance or characteristics of a desired partner. *This list is about the relationship you desire and how it functions.* Tap into your heart's desire and don't give any thought or attention to the qualities you don't want.

Writing Out Your Ideal Scenes

Now, write out two separate scenes that are evidence you've met your soulmate. For this exercise, *do not* include a proposal of marriage or a wedding; we would like you to picture something that would occur *before* those events. Leave out all physical characteristics of your beloved. Include the evidence that this person is someone you feel chemistry with, you have compatible lifestyles, shared values, and communication; all the evidence that this is your soulmate. These scenes shouldn't be sequential, with one leading to the other; instead, write out two scenes that occur separately and independently. Your scenes can be examples of one of your relationship values in action.

Ask yourself these questions:

- "What evidence would I need to know I'm with my beloved?"
- "What would that scene look like? Where is it taking place?"

Include as much detail as possible. Be specific, and incorporate all the details of your sensory experience: seeing, hearing, touching, smelling, and tasting. Incorporate your emotional states and where you feel them in your body. Write these scenes out in the present tense as if they're happening in the moment (not in the future). You may include what you're wearing, the weather, if you're having a meal what it smells and/or tastes like. Maybe it's an action your date is taking, or something they're saying, that indicates this person is your ideal match. Perhaps the circumstances in the scene reveal the evidence you require as well as the behavior of your beloved, or their response to you in a particular scenario.

After you've written your scenes, set them aside for a couple of days. Then select a day and time to do a ritual with them. You can light some candles or meditate before doing this ritual or put on some music or call in your guardian angels or spirit guides (whatever works for you to make it special). Feel all the good feelings as you're reading your ideal scenes out loud and visualize everything in your mind (all while leaving the details of your beloved's appearance unclear). The stronger attachment you create to your ideal scenes and the sensory experience of being with your soulmate, the more inspired you'll be to make it happen. Feel free to repeat the ritual of reading your ideal scenes as often as you like.

Scan the QR code for bonus materials and video trainings:

11

The Energetic Dance of Relationship

*"The positive and negative poles of a battery create an
electrical flow. The masculine and feminine poles between
people create a flow of sexual energy in motion."*
                                        —David Deida

The understanding of sexual orientation, gender, and identity has
changed dramatically in the last twenty years. While we applaud
this new understanding and sensitivity, we believe there needs to
be a new conversation around masculine and feminine energy and
how these energies interact in an intimate relationship. Tradition-
ally, masculine energy has been understood to be male and feminine energy has been understood to be female, when in truth,
every person has both masculine energy and feminine energy.
This distinction and gendered language is fraught with misunderstandings and questionable assumptions about gender and relationship roles. To create a new conversation about energetics and
how they play out in a romantic relationship (particularly through
the dating process), we'll be using new labels that better define
the roles and leave gender out of the conversation: leaders and
responders. The goal is to clear up confusion and uncertainty that
we've seen in the dating process for many singles who struggle to
find a soul-satisfying, long-lasting relationship regardless of gender identity and/or sexual orientation.

As every human contains both energies, they can draw upon them as needed. Some people are relatively balanced between the two, and others show a predominance of one of these energies; however, in each person, one energy is more dominant than the other. As you read these descriptions, ask yourself which energy feels more natural and genuine for you.

Leader energy is analytical, assertive, single-focused, and action-oriented. It's concerned more with doing than with being. You're most likely in your leader energy when you're at work and accomplishing goals. Leading energy moves with purpose and is competitive and logical. Being connected to your leader energy is essential for most occupations, as it encourages you to take charge, be productive, and achieve your goals. For leading energy to function and flourish, it needs to feel acknowledged and appreciated, admired, and needed. Leading energy dislikes being controlled or criticized. Put two leader energies together, and there's a natural competition that's born. In the positive, they hold each other accountable and strive to improve each other through challenges. In the negative, leader energy can be intent on winning, domination, and control.

Responder energy is inclusive, reflective, sensual, emotional, and reciprocal. It's great for creating connection and gathering information. Responder energy is intuitive, creative, and connected to flow. It's centered on being, as opposed to doing; there's space for allowing rather than a focus on goals and achievement. Responder energy needs to feel seen and protected in order to feel safe; it requires understanding, attention, and most of all, desires to be felt. Put two responder energies together, and there's a natural reciprocation and connection. In the positive, responder energy creates harmony and community. In the negative, it's passive, submissive, and lacks responsibility.

There is a natural dynamic to an intimate relationship that is unique. While romantic relationships have similarities to friendships, partnerships, and allies, the energetics of an intimate partnership are distinctive in that sexuality and chemistry are necessary. For example, two ballroom dancers are equal, but they don't provide the same steps to create a beautiful dance. Similar interests and backgrounds can help create a sense of comfort with a person but don't help determine whether the relationship can last. Having similar interests (or similar temperaments) is a recipe for a platonic friendship; the lack of polarity will limit attraction and the desire to have sex. To the dismay of all those who have failed at staying married to their best friend, attraction and passion don't develop because of similarities. Just as with magnets that have a North and South pole, the opposites are drawn to each other, while the same energies repel and therefore are not magnetic. Whether you decide to have children together or not, sex will be an essential element of your relationship. Your romantic partner is more than a roommate, a best friend, or someone who shares the domestic duties with you and helps raise the kids. Understanding the energetic dance of opposites, and the give and take between them, provides you with the secret for keeping attraction alive for a lifetime. It's chemistry and the desire for physical intimacy that puts gas in the tank of the relationship.

Attraction, sexual energy, and chemistry are created by opposing energies. It's the differences that fuel attraction, not your similarities; thus the colloquialism, "Opposites attract." Only by understanding this energetic dance of polarity can you feel comfortable in your own skin and create harmony in

Attraction, sexual energy, and chemistry are created by opposing energies. It's the differences that fuel attraction, not your similarities.

your love life. Rather than seeking a partner who's similar to you, you learn to respect and appreciate the differences between the two of you. This coming together of opposing energies is built into the survival of the human species. Two different people have diverse strengths and weaknesses, leveraging the ability of a couple to procreate and survive while safeguarding the family unit.

When you're considering which of these two energies best suits the relationship you're looking for, leader or responder, either select the energy that most resonates for you in the dating process or experiment with each energy with different dating partners and have fun discovering which one best aligns with your authentic self. These energetics are not set in stone; they become more fluid the longer you're in a relationship with the same person. Roles can switch over time, and both people can also move toward the center of these opposing poles. However, when you're dating, you'll want to choose one of these energetics from the start so that the relationship dynamic you desire is clearly established.

Deciding whether you're a leader or a responder at the start of the dating process with a prospect will ensure you never have to ask, "Where is this relationship going?" If you discover you have a pattern of wishing for the energetics to swap after several months, it's best to start over with a new prospect and choose the opposing energy to be dominant from the beginning. Flip-flopping from a leader to a responder will end up feeling like a bait-and-switch to that dating partner, and expecting them to go along with that energetic switch is an unrealistic expectation. That's why it's best to run the experiment when there's nothing at stake so you can discover your authentic disposition from the start. A person who presents as a leader at the start of the dating process but fades out by leaning back and not moving the relationship forward is a leader who is not ready for or interested in a committed relationship long-term. This is a leader who just wants companionship, a convenient relationship—more of a friends with benefits situation. Unfortunately, responders spend a lot of time trying to get these people to step up, which simply isn't possible. No one can make another person ready for a long-lasting love relationship. Spotting these people and moving on quickly will free your time (and your heart) to find someone who is an ideal match for you.

In a romantic partnership, leading and responding play off each other. Leaders provide a solid foundation and represent the roots and trunk of a tree, creating stability and certainty. Responders represent the leaves and flowers dancing in the wind producing joy. If you want to experience how leading and responding work together, take a ballroom dance class. Strong leading energy creates a solid foundation for responsive energy to express its creativity. When these energies are out of balance, then the relationship falls into dysfunction. Two leaders together will create an endless power struggle, and competition is the death of attraction. With two responders no one is leading, and you'll end up with a platonic friendship devoid of passion. All too often, responders present as leaders by showing off on a date rather than showing up emotionally present. These authentically responsive people end up confused as to why they struggle to create an emotional connection and don't end up with a request for a second or third date. Leaders who don't show their intention come across as passive and frustrate responders because they never move the relationship forward, creating insecurity and anxiety rather than emotional connection.

So how do you create an energetic balance in your relationship? The first step is to decide which energy turns you on. Are you more comfortable being the strong trunk of the tree, or do you want to dance in the wind? If you're unclear which energy feels right for you, you can conduct an experiment like our client Drew, a sweet, confident single man in his late 30s. Even though he's attractive, successful, and emotionally intelligent, he was perpetually single when he reached out to us. Being relationship-oriented and monogamous by nature, he wasn't comfortable with the hookup culture in his local gay community. When we discussed leading and responsive energy, he was unclear which role he preferred, so we gave him the assignment of choosing one energy as dominant for his different dating partners. We asked him to run an experiment to discover the difference in how he felt being a leader versus being a responder in the dating process. (FYI: This has nothing to do with how Drew showed up in other areas of his life.) On some dates, he'd pursue and take on the role of the leader; with others he'd relax into his responsive energy and let the other guy lead. Very quickly Drew realized that he felt insecure and anxious dating as the leader and much more comfortable and relaxed in the role of responder; it felt more natural for him. Once he made the choice to embrace his responsive energy through the dating process, he met a successful broker, and the two of them hit it off. Drew still runs his business, directs his staff, and spends his work hours primarily as a leader in his business. At home, he's the opposite, emphasizing receptivity, responsiveness, and nurturing his partner.

Following these practices will help you determine which energy is best aligned for your authentic self in a romantic relationship. Think about the role you wish to fulfill in your relationship and which role you'd like your partner to fulfill. If the idea of taking the lead in your relationship leaves you feeling tired, anxious, and wishing your partner would step up, relax into your responsive energy. If you feel energized and confident by driving the relationship forward and discovering how to bring more joy to your partner, embrace your leading energy. Relationships function best when there's a natural energetic polarity. This doesn't mean that there aren't times in your life and your relationship when you draw upon the opposing energy. Remember, every person has both leading and responsive energies.

Embracing the Responder

Corrine sat next to an attractive man on a plane; the two of them quickly hit it off flirting, and it was clear he was interested in her. Upon landing, he offered to take her bag down from the overhead bin, but she insisted that she get it herself. They walked off the plane together and discovered they were both heading to the same terminal for a connecting flight, and he once again offered help with her carry-on bag. She confidently told him that she had it handled. She noticed a change in him, and even though they continued walking together, he didn't ask for her number when they parted. Corrine knew she'd missed a great opportunity but wasn't sure what had gone wrong. While telling us about their exchange, she realized that by refusing his assistance she'd made it clear that there wasn't any room for him to be helpful. She had energetically shown up in her leading energy, which is a turn-off to a man who wants to provide something to a woman he's romantically interested in.

Relaxing into your responsive energy can happen in a moment by allowing yourself to receive. Responsive and receptive energy is not passive or weak. Being conscious of how you're showing up in the world and taking specific actions to shift your energy, you can quickly learn to step into your personal power and inspire the person you're dating to step up for you and lead.

Camille was frustrated with her dating life. She'd quickly invest emotionally with guys who later revealed themselves to be flaky and emotionally unavailable. She couldn't figure out how to break this pattern. In talking with her, we discovered with all these experiences she was the one moving the relationship forward. When she liked a guy, she'd ask him out for a second date, and then she was usually initiating communication as well as meeting up in person. She had made it easy and convenient for these guys to spend time with her, thus concealing the fact that they weren't emotionally available for a committed relationship. With our guidance, Camille slowed down in the dating process, and instead of taking charge of the situation she'd sit back and let the prospect lead. Quickly she met one man who behaved very differently than all her other prospects. He'd reach out in advance to schedule the next date, always made sure her water glass was full at a restaurant, and made future plans for a trip with her. It surprised Camille how quickly her energetic shift while dating produced the desired results. This particular guy wasn't a good match for a long-term relationship; however, he was great practice for her to become comfortable allowing her responder energy to be dominant. She's no longer wasting time with guys who ghost her as soon as it gets complicated; she's feeling comfortable in her own skin and is no longer overcome with anxiety.

Embracing responsive energy is easy when you hone these qualities: in touch with your emotional life, sensory experience, connecting with nature, and accessing your creativity. You can also create a ritual to step into being responsive. Listen to music that relaxes you, put on some perfume, light a scented candle, or dress in an outfit that makes you feel sexy in order to shift your energy from getting things done to connecting with your sensory experience.

Responsive energy has a deep connection to creativity. Connecting to your creative side gets you out of your analytical, logical mind and into the flow of your creativity. Spend some time writing poetry or song lyrics, sing along to your favorite song, or get your coloring pencils or paints out. There are apps you can add to your mobile phone that allow you to throw pottery on a wheel, color in a mandala, or paint like a pro. Bake something tasty or cook up a delicious meal. Your creative energy is innately responsive and connected to your sensory experience—no overthinking is required.

Practice being receptive. Unfortunately, many responders can have a tough time receiving, as they've been conditioned to believe that their worth comes from their ability to get things done. Accept a compliment without reciprocating, and welcome offers of help and support instead of showing off how capable you are. It's not weak to accept help when offered, especially when you're learning to relax into being responsive. Just say, "Thank you," when someone compliments you instead of downplaying yourself or reciprocating by offering a compliment back. The more you practice receiving, the more you tap into your receptive energy and leave opportunities for a leader to step up for you.

Get in the habit of filling your own cup first. Sacrifice and self-abandonment are negative aspects of the responder. Just like accepting help doesn't mean you're not capable or weak, filling your cup first doesn't mean you're selfish or uncaring. Your self-care routine supports your responsive energy—something as simple as self-reflection, journaling, yoga, a warm bubble bath, or whatever you do to refresh and refuel. Creating a habit of self-care activities ensures you won't take on too much or run on empty. When you take care of yourself, you can cultivate connection rather than competition.

Remember, responsive energy is naturally reciprocal, and leading energy is competitive. Connection creates understanding, empathy, compassion, and community. When you're connected to yourself, you're able to authentically connect with someone else. Embrace the power of the responder by showing up instead of showing off. Showing up is about authenticity, presence, listening, responding, or redirecting. The role of the responder is to let the leader know the water is warm (that you're interested), to flirt, and to respond to their advances. Responders can slow down the pace of a relationship and also have veto power. Rather than rejecting a leader outright for wanting to move the relationship forward faster than you care for, see if you can redirect to a pace you're more comfortable with.

Embracing the Leader

Sean hadn't been dating for some time after his divorce and lacked confidence in his ability to meet someone. He liked to keep his intentions hidden and instead waited to see if the woman he was dating would take the lead. After several dates with Andrea, he told us he didn't want to date anyone else but didn't plan on telling her. He wanted to stick to his past dating approach and follow her lead, waiting to see where the relationship went. We encouraged him to share his feelings and to take a risk by asking Andrea to go exclusive with him. As his resistance continued, we reminded him to step into his leader energy and be more intentional in his approach to dating and not just leave it all up to chance. He paused a moment and thoughtfully said with a laugh, "I have a whole new understanding of what you mean by Creating Love on Purpose." He took the uncomfortable step of declaring his intention and claiming his leader energy to enter an exclusive relationship with Andrea. To his delight, she was thrilled he asked her, and his self-confidence grew by taking a risk and claiming Andrea as his girlfriend.

Remember, it's the polarity of the energetics that creates the spark of attraction which is essential for lasting love. Leading and responding are the polarity of energies that must be present for the dance of relationship. It's important for leaders to step up and declare their truth; risk to discover whether the other person is on the same page and interested in a relationship. There's a reason why in every romantic comedy at some point the leader makes a speech about what they want and how the responder fulfills their vision of an ideal mate. Harry declares at the end of *When Harry Met Sally*, "I came here tonight because when you realize you want to spend the rest of your life with somebody you want the rest of your life to start as soon as possible." It's a big romantic gesture to declare your intentions in a relationship. Leading energy is about owning your truth and declaring it to the world. Embracing it requires you to know and trust yourself, instead of hesitating and expecting the other person to take the lead.

Lead, but also be flexible. Responders may offer a counter proposal and make a request or use their veto power outright. Allow space to adjust to the responder you find attractive. Rigidity and stubbornness are negative aspects of leading energy. Have a direction and a goal in mind while also being open to feedback—this is how the dance of leaders and responders functions in harmony together. In order to stand in your leading energy, discover what grounds you in your power. Whether it's weight training or martial arts (or whatever physical discipline stimulates you), leaders are fed by tapping into physical power and strength. This doesn't mean you're required to be good at sports or to compete; rather, it's that you're connected to the physical power of your body, and you use that to ground yourself and boost self-confidence.

Having single-pointed focus is a strength of the leader, and meditation allows you to develop this skill by helping you focus your attention so that you can quiet your mind. Focus and concentration are required to accomplish tasks and achieve your goals. Seek healthy competition in order to improve and become a superior person. Competition sometimes gets a bad rap, but it's essential to sharpen skills and become extraordinary (like King Arthur's knights of the Round Table). Search for the company of positive role models who can hold you accountable and inspire you to do better. Healthy competition builds confidence and self-esteem, helps develop problem-solving skills and discipline, and reduces stress. Leaders often compete in groups to improve and grow into better individuals as steel sharpens steel. This dynamic is imperative for leaders to thrive in all areas of their life.

Staying in your integrity gives you a foundation to stand on, builds lasting trust with your partner, and guides you when challenges arise. Integrity doesn't mean you won't make mistakes, but it allows you to take responsibility for them and to make amends if necessary. Gender roles in traditional marriages placed the husband in the role of financial provider, while the wife took care of the home and raised the children. This arrangement no longer applies to most marriages in the twenty-first century. Many women are the breadwinners while many men stay at home and raise the children. However, the role of the provider is important for leading energy, so it's important to know what you provide to your partner and family (particularly when it's not financial). Providing for responders brings safety, security, and increases joy. Whether it's emotional support, financial support, trust, security, acceptance, space for the responder in your life to feel and express, or a safe place to land, knowing what you provide gives you the confidence to wisely choose a life partner. Having strength and confidence allows you to share your vulnerability without fear of being perceived as weak; there's nothing feeble about vulnerability. Compassion, empathy, and acceptance keep the leader in balance and in harmony with their life partner. In the dating process, the role of the leader is to move the relationship forward, declare your intentions, and adjust to the responder in order to ensure their happiness.

* * *

Before entering into your next relationship, introspect about your comfort level with leading and responding. Ask yourself which of these two energies feels more natural for you. Are you the leader, or would you rather respond? Who would you rather partner with, the leader or the responder? Which energy do you find most attractive? Once you have clarity, commit to your chosen energy. If you want someone to step up and claim you, don't show up and compete with your date; instead, share your emotional authenticity and make requests. If you see yourself taking the lead, don't abdicate your power by constantly looking for approval; instead, declare your intentions and let the chips fall where they may. Embracing the energetic dance of leaders and responders will clear up the confusion through the dating process so you can find an ideal mate for life.

Embracing the energetic dance of leaders and responders will clear up confusion through the dating process so you can find an ideal mate for life.

There's nothing better than real life to provide a clear understanding of these energetics in action. While driving home from work our client Cami was speaking with Joaquin, who she hadn't been dating very long. At one point she casually mentioned that one of her tires was low on air and the car was beeping to notify her about it. Joaquin asked if she was heading home, and she told him she planned to go for a walk before dinner. That's when he asked if he could bring over his air compressor and fill up the tire. Then they could go for a walk together and he'd like to take her to dinner too (if she wasn't already booked with another engagement). As he was getting out of his car in her driveway, Cami thanked him for going out of his way to help her. "Well of course, I want to be your hero!" he exclaimed. Eventually, they went exclusive on Valentine's Day, and within two years they got married. Cami had never been a bride before and, now over sixty, is sharing the best years of her life with her beloved husband. He still makes sure everything in and around the house is in good working order, and he's still going out of his way to increase her happiness. With time Joaquin has shown Cami he's capable of meeting her needs, allowing her to relax, worry less, and let him handle things she dislikes or isn't very good at. She had never imagined that life with a partner could be so easy and drama free.

LOVE ON PURPOSE EXERCISE—GIVING AND RECEIVING

This journaling exercise helps you get clear on the energetic dynamic you desire in an intimate relationship. The bad math of an unhealthy relationship is 1+1=1 or "you complete me." Our bad relationship math is 1+1=3, two whole and complete people come together and create a new entity, the relationship. Part of being in a relationship is making deposits and withdrawals from the relationship instead of overgiving or selfishly taking from your partner.

Start by journaling about what you bring to a relationship. What would your partner expect to receive from you? You can write about positive qualities you have, benefits your partner would get from you, and why they'd be interested in you. Don't focus on external qualities like your looks or your income (although they could be included); instead, write about the intangible qualities that make you a good partner. On a separate page, journal about what you expect to receive in your relationship. What do you expect your partner to bring to you? Once again, focus on the intangible qualities over the tangible ones. This isn't a list of qualities that you expect your partner to bring; it's about the dynamic between the two of you.

Next, find a place to sit quietly and read through these pages a couple of times. Now that you've got a firm grip on the dynamic you desire in your intimate relationship, close your eyes and imagine a ball of light in the center of your chest. This is your intention of what you bring. Breathe into that ball of light, and as you exhale, imagine that light being sent out into the world and landing on different people and places. As that intention is received, now imagine that light returning to you as the recipient has received your message and responds with their desire to give you all that you desire. After this process, reflect on what it feels like to know that your message was received and that your future partner is out there waiting for you to find them. How will you move through the world differently, knowing it's just a matter of time before you meet your soulmate?

Scan the QR code for bonus materials and video trainings:

12

Soulmating

"We are all a little weird and life's a little weird, and when we find someone whose weirdness is compatible with ours, we join up with them and fall in mutual weirdness and call it love."

—Dr. Seuss

Anhe didn't like the uncertainty of dating. When a guy she liked asked her out for a second date, she would deactivate her dating profile and focus only on him. A few years after her coaching program with us was completed, Anhe reached out to us to get a refresher on the dating strategies we taught her. She sheepishly told us she hadn't followed our recommendations and had spent the last few years going out with one person for three to six months, having it end, feeling heartbroken, spending some time on her own, and then going back into the dating pool. Her longest relationship was eight months, and she was feeling frustrated that none of her connections led to a longer commitment. Nothing had changed with her dating life despite the inner shifts she had experienced. We encouraged her to delay exclusivity, use the dating process to discover more about herself, and practice all the tools and resources we'd given her. Anhe committed to dating our way regardless of how uncomfortable it felt. She confessed that she'd been longing to find someone to love her, yet she had no clue how to love herself. Her love imprint, "I am invisible," was a self-fulfilling prophecy that seemed to dictate the end of every relationship before it could even get started. With our recommendation, she pledged to schedule weekly Inner Child Dates to create a new connection with the little girl inside of her and to delay exclusivity even when she felt a spark with someone.

As an Asian woman, Anhe was highly concerned about how a guy would react when she told him she was going to continue seeing other people. We assured her that it's not unique to the Asian community to only date one person at a time (whether it's spoken and agreed to or not); there are plenty of other cultures where exclusivity is expected when two people like each other and agree to date. However, when she was authentic and shared her new dating strategies with potential partners, she would utilize social pressure to her advantage. By stating her intention of wanting to date several people at a time upfront, she reduced the likelihood of reverting back to committing to one person quickly. Social pressure doesn't have to always be a bad thing; when you're looking to break a bad habit, announcing your objective to other people at the start sets you up for success. If Anhe's old dating style was going to work for her, it would have by now; she had nothing to lose and everything to gain.

Speaking her truth and evaluating herself through the dating process started to build her confidence (along with weekly Inner Child Dates). Comparing how she felt with one guy versus another gave her the perspective that she needed to cultivate discernment and evaluate the guys she was dating in an entirely new way. We promised Anhe that the cream always rises to the top, and sure enough one particular man stood out over time. Moving slower than she'd ever imagined, they eventually started dating exclusively, met each other's families, were engaged, and got married. Her true soul partnership didn't occur at breakneck speed because Anhe needed to discover how to make her own needs a priority before she could show someone else how to love her. They're still happily married years later, and Anhe continues the ritual of weekly Inner Child Dates to nurture her relationship with herself.

In addition to the myth of love by accident, there's another reason most people rush through dating to a commitment. Most people don't sit down and craft a vision of their true soul partnership *before* they start dating. Instead, they wait and see how it goes, expecting to know it when they see it. As you've come to realize, this a recipe for allowing Your Love Imprint to select your partner. We call this "I'll know it when I see it" approach "dating backward." One of the biggest mistakes people make while dating is to give the benefit of the doubt to a stranger (because they feel attraction and chemistry) and then once they're in a committed relationship, they take off their rose-colored glasses only to find fault and disappointment with their partner. Dating backward includes the unrealistic expectation that you'll never have conflict with the "right person," or have to speak up and make a request because the "right person" will just know what you prefer. The sensation of falling in love is a chemical high that leads you to falsely believe that the romance stage will never end. Eventually that chemical high will wear off, and you're left with a person who you thought initially was just like you and wanted the same things in life as you, and now you're seeing them as different than you and conflicts begin to arise. Creating Love on Purpose means that you're purposeful every step of the way. It still includes all the romance, butterflies in your stomach, and excitement, without all the angst, uncertainty,

Creating Love on Purpose means that you're purposeful every step of the way.

and eventual sorrow and heartbreak you've experienced from a love imprint match.

To get off the rollercoaster of hope, to expectation, to disappointment in your love life, we want you to first use the dating process as an experiment to discover about yourself. We call this process Dating to Discover, our process for avoiding dating burnout and speeding up the time it takes to meet your person. You'll learn how to develop your dating discernment so you can choose the right partner and stop leaving your love life to chance. Dating to Discover puts the focus on you first because you're the common denominator in all your relationships. It doesn't matter who's sitting across from you; your patterns and strategies will reveal themselves. Plus, you are the only person in charge of your love life—no one else is going to do it for you. Using these practices gives you a new perspective on dating, so that your time isn't wasted whether the date goes well or not. Every date is an opportunity to discover about yourself and practice being authentic—so no date is a waste of time. You'll continue to use all these new skills, exercises, and strategies through the dating process, going exclusive and committing to a life together and throughout your entire relationship.

Imagine that you're in a dating lab, and your goal is to simply collect data. In order to do that, you'll have to go on a lot of dates with different kinds of people. Attraction is a requirement for a relationship, but it's *not* essential for a date. Set the bar for a first meet really, really low. "Not an ax murderer," is the kind of low bar we're asking you to set. This isn't to torture you but to expand what's possible for you in love. When you're super selective about meeting someone for a date you're more likely to just repeat your negative patterns again and again. The impulse to let your heart decide right off the bat without enough data and absent enough comparisons means you'll most likely fall for the false positive of Your Love Imprint. No point in doing that again, right?

Ideally, go on two to three dates a week. Beware of guarding your time as an excuse for guarding your heart. Early dates don't have to be long drawn-out events. Instead, think of the first couple of dates as casual meetings to get to know each other. You can even string together two to three first meets on a Saturday or Sunday; you're in control of the types of dates and durations that work best for your schedule. You can save time by not playing private investigator googling your potential matches. Just go meet with whoever asks for about an hour, ninety minutes max. Don't spend a lot of time in long drawn-out text or virtual communications with someone you haven't yet met. Get to that first in-person meeting as quickly as possible. If you can't make time in your schedule to date, then you might not have time for an actual relationship. When you're serious about finding lasting love, dating different people with regularity is an important part of the process.

Beware of guarding your time as an excuse for guarding your heart.

Resistance to dating is one of the top blocks to love. Expecting to magically meet your person without investing time dating before exclusivity leaves you without a plan for love. A first meet is just that; you'll want to see them face-to-face and leave them wanting more. Make plans after your first dates so you have somewhere to go. According to Lisa Gaeta, the CEO of Impact Personal Safety in Los Angeles, you should "practice safety when going on first dates. Someone looking to do harm will take you from your original meeting place to another location." When it comes to first dates, avoid suggesting going to a second location, and avoid saying "yes" to someone offering it. This person is a stranger, and it's imperative you put your safety first. If this is your beloved, you'll have plenty of time to spend together—the rest of your lives. Another reason to set the bar low is that you never know where or how you'll meet your soulmate. One of Orna's closest friends from UCLA is married to the brother of a guy Orna met on JDate. Spending an hour with someone you don't hit it off with is not a waste of your time; it's an excellent opportunity to practice being authentic with nothing at stake.

Let's take a look at common dating mistakes before we set you up for dating success. The most common is rushing to exclusivity before knowing if lifestyle and life goals are a match. Most people dislike dating and think of it as a necessary evil, and they rely solely on chemistry and attraction, ignoring possible red flags. Two typical strategies that lead people astray are being so particular that no one measures up, or being so easygoing that they sacrifice their needs by going along to get along—two very different strategies with the same end result. With online dating, there's an exaggerated fear of being scammed, too little effort in creating an online profile, and looking for a soulmate in a profile (as if it's possible to identify energetics in an app). Once you start dating, popular mistakes include showing off instead of showing up, treating dates like a job interview with preselected questions, putting your self-esteem and lovability in the hands of a stranger, and finally creating an extensive list of qualities and rejecting anyone who doesn't fit the list to a T. These pitfalls are easy to avoid simply by using better dating strategies and by being authentic (which you've already been practicing). Ninety-eight percent of the time a client emails us with a question of what to do during the dating process the answer is, "Use the Speak How You Feel Template." If you want a shift in your dating life, practice the SHYFT and use it liberally.

Upon assigning Dating to Discover to a client, she was dismayed at the prospect of telling strangers her feelings. "Won't I just be annoying people by complaining all the time?" she asked pointedly. The assumption that she would be only sharing her *negative* emotions is certainly illuminating. Speaking how you feel doesn't just mean you speak up when you're feeling upset or need to clear something up. It's appropriate for you to share your feelings at any time with anyone. The right match for you will want to know how you feel. They'll want to know what pleases you and brings you joy. If you're the kind of person who holds their cards close to their chest, it's time to break that habit. You won't suddenly start expressing yourself five years into a marriage; it's important you start practicing now—*before* you meet your beloved.

Dating to Discover

Now let's take a look at how to implement slow love with our step-by-step protocol for dating to meet your soulmate.

Principle Number One—Go on a lot of dates! Exactly how many dates is not a specific number; however, it's essential you gather enough data by going on dates with multiple people. You can think of it as a dating rotation. Most people let their inherent biases get in the way of meeting someone new. They spend their time wading through profiles looking for reasons to say "no": too short, wrong color hair, no college degree, standing in front of a sports car, we've heard it all. Look for reasons to say "yes" instead. Stop creating barriers to meeting new people. Every person you meet is a chance to learn more about yourself, to get a clearer picture of what you want in a beloved partnership, and to be authentic and practice making requests. The idea is to get as much data from the dating lab as you can. The more data you can collect about your habitual thought patterns, emotional triggers, and limiting beliefs, the more ways you can adjust your mindset and approach to finding a life partner. It's on you to remain positive and optimistic throughout your journey.

Principle Number Two—Place your attention on self-discovery. It doesn't matter how much self-growth work you've already done, or how much therapy, or how many relationships you've had. Whether you're thirty or seventy years old, age doesn't matter. The discovery process through dating is rich with information regarding your current blocks to love. Resist the urge to evaluate if the person is a match for you or not until after five to six dates. Instead, put the focus on you and see what you can discover about yourself. While five to six dates per prospect might seem like a lot, the truth is when you're authentic, someone who's not a match will deselect themselves. It's actually rare to make all the way to five or six dates with someone you're not interested in before they deselect themselves. The only caveat to this is if there's a genuine deal-breaker present. Run the celebrity crush exercise (at the end of this chapter) to determine if it's really a point of issue for you in a relationship. You'll be provided with a breakup script (deselection script) so you'll be able to keep your heart karma clean. Dating with integrity means no ghosting and utilizing the SHYFT with regularity.

There's zero risk practicing being authentic and using the SHYFT while dating. Your intention is to discover how you show up differently with different people. Is it easy to be authentic when you don't find your date attractive? What's different about your behavior and your inner dialog when your date is hot or you sense a connection? It's very important to take note of your feeling state during and immediately after a date. Are you looking for clues in order to win their affection or approval? Are you going along to get along and not expressing your values? We have a rate-your-date journal for you at the end of this chapter to help you track your dating.

Principle Number Three—Attraction is *not* a requirement for a date. Chemistry and attraction are a necessary ingredient for a *relationship*, but not at all for a date. It's just a date—not a commitment to spend your life with this person. To truly put yourself in the dating lab, you'll need to collect data on your dating strategies and behaviors through many different experiences with a lot of different people. Going on a date with someone you are *not* attracted to is how you'll make some of your

> *Chemistry and attraction are a necessary ingredient for a relationship, but not at all for a date.*

best discoveries that will lead you to your soulmate. We're not suggesting you get into a committed relationship with someone you don't find attractive—quite the opposite. Never settle when it comes to a committed relationship, but a date is only an hour or two out of your life. Letting go of the need to find the spark of attraction as a prerequisite for a date will bring you many more opportunities to go on a lot more dates. This allows you to evaluate yourself from an entirely new perspective—one that will ultimately lead you to creating a long-lasting, healthy, and thriving relationship. When you're not attracted to your date, you'll let go of unrealistic expectations and you'll have permission to be unapologetically you. The goal of dating is finding the person who wants *you*, not for companionship or convenience for right now. This is how you find a partner who gets you, who claims you, who will ultimately stand by you no matter what.

Principle Number Four—Choose to date from either leader energy or responder energy through the dating process. The person who desires to be primarily in their leader energy in the relationship is tasked with moving the relationship forward. The person who wishes to be primarily in their responder energy in the relationship is responsive.

Responders, as long as you're being asked out again, we ask that you go on five to six dates before deselecting anyone. This will give you an immense amount of exploration and training to practice the SHYFT and make requests. Leaders, resist the urge to stop dating anyone else because you're hot for someone. You cannot go exclusive and just not tell the other person. Even worse is asking someone to go exclusive after one or two dates. There's so much breadth and depth to your relationship with yourself that we're asking you not to short-change yourself. Regardless of gender or sexual orientation, have a rotation so you can be in the dating lab. One of our male clients who dates men put in his online profile that he's put himself in the dating lab and wants to meet in person ASAP. When we suggested this to a female client who was having trouble being asked out by men online, she suddenly had many dates lined up in advance.

Principle Number Five—Delay exclusivity. You can start evaluating if the other person is a match for you after date five or six, but we don't recommend rushing to take yourself off the market. The right match for you will be patient, honor your requests, and strive to win your heart. If someone doesn't wait for you, then they're not a good match for you long-term anyway. Putting off exclusivity allows you to evaluate your dates for who they really are instead of through the rose-colored glasses of excitement. Date *without* the rose-colored glasses and set them aside for later on when you've agreed to share the rest of your lives together; by then they've earned the benefit of the doubt. Never give a stranger the benefit of the doubt. Extending grace with your soulmate is a skill that's required for love to last and stand the test of time. Additionally, putting off exclusivity will mean you'll no longer have a bunch of short-term relationships. This speeds up the process of recognizing a soulmate through the dating process. You'll date multiple people for a longer time and only go off the market for the person who's making an effort to win your heart.

Principle Number Six—Delay physical intimacy until exclusivity. Dating for your soulmate relationship means that you're delaying sexual relations with a prospect until there's an agreement and a conversation about exclusivity. This is important because when you orgasm, your brain can release oxytocin, which is a bonding hormone. For most people, sex creates feelings of emotional connection and intimacy; creating the illusion of that connection takes your brain offline for the selection process. Having sex before exclusivity increases the chance of becoming emotionally attached before you know if they are an ideal long-term partner. If you're looking to date causally or explore your sexuality and your goal is not a long-term monogamous relationship, have all the sex you like. However, becoming physically intimate quickly most often translates to an imbalanced dynamic in the relationship where one person wants a friends with benefits or hookup arrangement and the other desires exclusivity. When there's high chemistry, it's incredibly titillating to wait. It's all in how you do it. Not because we're asking you to date like it's 1952, but rather so you can make a conscious decision about who you're physically intimate with before you bond emotionally with them.

If someone is moving toward physical intimacy faster than you're comfortable with, you can slow them down by saying, "It'll be hot when we do, but I'm not ready yet." "Not yet" is the key to let someone know you're interested in them but not ready for physical intimacy. There's no set rule on when to have sex in a relationship. The only rule to abide by is that you have a conversation about what sex means to you *before* you engage. When there are differing expectations of what sex means but you don't have a conversation about it, you're setting yourself up for misunderstandings, a blow to your self-esteem, and potential heartbreak. Keep your sanity and your ability to decipher how you feel without bringing sex into the picture too early. You'll thank us later when you're spending the rest of your life with the love of your life.

There's no set rule on when to have sex in a relationship. The only rule to abide by is that you have a conversation about what sex means to you before you engage.

Principle Number Seven—Track your dating progress. This is the roadmap to recognize your soulmate. Utilizing the dating process to discover about yourself first; you'll uncover things you never considered before, including but not limited to, additional details of the vision of your ideal relationship and how it functions. How do you feel when you spend time with this person? How do the two of you navigate miscommunication or disagreements? How do they respond to you when you've been triggered or upset? How do the two of you reconnect and repair after there's been a dispute? Are they accommodating or demanding? Your answers to these questions are the important foundation of the vision that will ultimately guide you to recognizing your soulmate out in the world. This is much more indicative of a lasting partnership than looking for someone who enjoys the same kinds of music and hobbies as you, or letting your emotions or hormones choose for you. Don't shy away from uncomfortable conversations through the dating process. You'll learn more about yourself and the potential of your date when you can risk and speak up about what's important to you. Utilize the SHYFT to discover if the person you're dating has the capacity to meet your needs.

Principle Number Eight—Look for someone who's a match to your values. Connecting with someone who has the same values as you makes that person a candidate for a long-term match. Through the dating process, you'll want to notice how your date spends their resources: time, energy, and money. This will reveal to you what they truly value in life. As we discussed in Chapter Ten, values are something you discover as you spend quality time together. Having shared values creates longevity in an intimate relationship. You can always find your way back to each other no matter the challenge because you both have the same priorities. Ultimately, the dating process is a selection process, and it's just as important to know who to deselect as it is to select. Dating with our tried-and-true strategies will invigo-rate your dating process because you'll never waste time on short-term, dead-end relationships that send you back to the dating pool over and over again, causing you to feel burned out and frustrated with the whole process.

Having shared values creates longevity in an intimate relationship. You can always find your way back to each other no matter the challenge because you both have the same priorities.

Laleh became our client after an ugly breakup with a fiancé she'd caught cheating. She had spent sev-eral years healing her heart and tak-ing care of herself and was ready to start dating again. After laying out our dating practices, she came to the next session with this question, "Do I have to go out with this unattractive guy that just asked me out?" "Yes!" we chimed in unison, "What do you have to lose?" We could feel her eye roll through the telephone. After some encouragement that attraction is not a requirement for a date, she reluctantly agreed to just discover about herself through the dating process. In all Laleh went out with Dion for five dates, and for the first time she experienced how a man behaves when he's invested in getting to know her. Her lack of attraction didn't change, but she was treated with a level of interest and kindness she'd never experienced before. Dion packed a picnic with all of Laleh's favorite things, includ-ing a nice bottle of wine (half of the items she didn't specifically remember ever telling him about). He bought tickets to a con-cert for a band she'd always wanted to see live. With every inter-action he was chivalrous and a consummate gentleman. When she broke it off with him, he thanked her by saying, "I don't know why you let me take you out on so many dates when you're clearly out of my league. I've had such a good time getting to know you. Thank you!" Laleh finally understood what she was looking for—a man who would make an effort to win her heart.

As an attractive woman, Laleh always dated very attractive men, and handsome men don't usually have to work hard to get dates. The experience of dating Dion changed her outlook on the dating process altogether. Now she was eager to set the bar low and just meet with whoever wanted to take her out. No date is a waste of your time and energy if you're invested in discovering about yourself. Every dating experience comes with a treasure trove of learning if you're willing to remain in curiosity. Before long Lelah met the man who would eventually become her husband, and as we had promised she found him highly attractive from the start. Committing to date without the expectation of finding your soulmate takes pressure off the dating process as well as the analysis paralysis that comes with setting the bar high. As counterintuitive as it may seem, moving slowly through the dating process speeds up meeting your soulmate.

LOVE ON PURPOSE EXERCISES

Now that you're ready to enter the dating lab, here are the tools you'll need to evaluate and track your progress. The rate-your-date journal allows you to evaluate your progress through the dating process. The celebrity crush exercise brings clarity to your deal-breakers in relationship. Finally, the break-up script gives you the words to respectfully deselect a prospect when it's clear they aren't a match for you.

Rate-Your-Date Journal

To get better at anything you'll need a metric to show your improvement, and you're now in a position to track your dating. The entire dating process can be a great way to discover more about yourself and give you an opportunity to practice the SHYFT as well as your other new tools and strategies with nothing at stake. This will also help you to create a clearer vision of the kind of relationship you want *before* attempting to select a partner.

Complete this exercise after every date. Track the answers as you continue to date multiple people as well as date the same person again and again. This will give you important insights into your own emotional and behavioral patterns. Pay close attention if you're showing up differently based on the level of attraction you feel toward a date.

1. Score yourself on a scale of 1–10 on how authentic you were able to be on the date, with 1 being not at all and 10 being one hundred percent authentic.

2. Were you attracted to your date? Score your level of attraction on a scale of 1–10, with 1 being no attraction and 10 being highest level of attraction.

3. Did your level of attraction affect your ability to be authentic and speak how you feel or make a request?

4. What were your primary emotions on the date?

5. How did you feel when you immediately parted from the date?

6. Could you identify your inner dialog? What were you saying to yourself about yourself?

7. Did your date inspire kind and loving thoughts about yourself? Or did your date inspire critical, judgmental thoughts?

8. Was there a missed opportunity to speak up or make a request when you did not?

9. Did you ignore any possible conflicts and attempt to be accommodating? Or were you able to speak up when there was an issue that needed to be addressed?

10. Are there any things you wish you would have done differently on the date? How might you change your approach moving forward?

Clarifying Your Deal-Breakers—Celebrity Crush Exercise

Most singles are hyper-concerned about deal-breakers when they're dating. It's as if they want to make sure there are no loopholes to squeak in some characteristics they don't want in a partner. Making a long list of deal-breakers is another way that people focus on avoiding the pain from past experiences in love. It's also how people end up drawing in a potential match with similar issues, making it easy to repeat a negative pattern.

Once you know your specific deal-breakers, you won't have to put any energy into characteristics you don't want. You'll know who to deselect in the dating process and who to continue to be curious about. Your list of deal-breakers doesn't have to include universal qualities that are the foundation of a loving partnership for everyone, like no cheaters, liars, abusers, and so on. Your list of deal-breakers is personal to you. They might be perfectly acceptable or desirable characteristics for someone else. (Smoking is a great example; it's a deal-breaker for some people and a desired common habit for others.)

Here's our fun and foolproof way to get crystal clear on your deal-breakers: First, pick a person to be your celebrity crush. This person can be anyone: an actor, author, singer, poet, or any type of public figure. This isn't someone you fancy and just want to have sex with, this is someone you imagine is your ideal match for a long-term, committed relationship. And of course, you find them hot!

Now, select a quality you think is a deal-breaker for you. Sticking with the example of smoking cigarettes, imagine you meet your celebrity crush and they're into you and want a relationship with you—but they smoke. If you'd give your celebrity crush a pass on smoking cigarettes, then you have to give a pass to Joe Schmoe/Jane Doe as well because it's not *really* a deal-breaker. If you'll make an exception for your celebrity crush, then you must make the exception with *everyone*. With a genuine deal-breaker you wouldn't even give your celebrity crush a pass on.

Go ahead and make your new list of deal-breakers and ask yourself if your celebrity crush could get away with each characteristic. If yes, then cross it out and take it off the list. You may find your new list is shorter than the original one because you've clarified what's really important to you as opposed to those things that your ex did that annoyed you but really aren't deal-breakers with your person. There's no specific number of deal-breakers; your list is unique to you. Someone who is very religious and rather conservative may have a lot more than someone who is not. This is not a cookie-cutter exercise, and there's no one size fits most.

Once you know your actual deal-breakers you won't deselect people willy-nilly, based on your mood that particular day. One of our clients always thought she wanted to have children and she deselected guys that were not interested in having them over and over right from the start. When she completed this celebrity crush exercise she discovered that she'd forgo kids with her celebrity crush, which means it's not *actually* a deal-breaker. Her dating strategies completely changed. Deselecting guys that didn't want to have kids had kept her heart safe, so safe she was still single into her forties.

Tapping into your list of genuine deal-breakers puts you in the seat of your power through the dating process because you don't have to place emphasis on the qualities you're not looking for in an ideal mate.

The Breakup Script

Letting someone know that you're no longer interested in dating them can be awkward. This is why so many people just disappear and ghost. If you've ever had this happen to you, then you know how awful it feels to be left wondering what happened. Instead of ghosting someone or stumbling through a text exchange, or even worse a runaway conversation that leaves you both feeling bad, we're giving you a template for a mature and respectful dialog to moving on. Here's how to deselect someone you've been dating.

First option: Meet them for a scheduled date and use the script right at the start. Don't go on a date with someone and then at the end of an evening together deselect them.

Second option: Speak on the phone and deselect using the script. Never deliver this script via text message or any text communication like email.

Breakup script: "I am aware of the kind of relationship I am looking for, and it is clear to me that we are not a match. I know that your ideal match is out there, and I wish you the best of luck in your search for love."

Dating like a grown-up means you can treat someone respectfully and end the dating process. It's important that you're sincere about the words you're saying and that you truly wish them luck on their journey. There's no need to elaborate further. If pressed with questions, you can rest assured this is further proof this person is not a long-term match. You're under no obligation to answer them; it's best not to open up a dialog regarding your desires. There's nothing more that needs to be said beyond the breakup script.

Scan the QR code for bonus materials and video trainings:

13

The Five Stages of Relationship

"Find the person who will love you because of your differences and not in spite of them, and you have found a lover for life."

—Leo Buscaglia

A romantic, intimate relationship can be one of the most potent personal growth journeys you'll ever experience—one that heals your wounds and stands as a safe harbor when difficulties arise. Knowing the natural progression of a romantic partnership allows you to adjust your strategies and expectations and gives you a recipe for long-lasting love. Couples therapist and author Dr. Susan Campbell studied over one hundred couples and discovered that intimate relationships transform through five stages, and each stage requires you to adjust and grow for love to continue to blossom. Seen through this lens, your relationship becomes the ultimate tool for your own personal and spiritual growth, as well as strengthening the connection with your partner, allowing your love for each other to grow deeper.

> *A romantic, intimate relationship can be one of the most potent personal growth journeys you'll ever experience—one that heals your wounds and stands as a safe harbor when difficulties arise.*

Once you decide on exclusivity, an awareness of the five stages of relationship helps you discover over time if you've found an ideal match for long-lasting love. Be open and curious of your partner's ability to navigate these stages with you, or not. You'll be able to quickly move on and take your knowledge with you (and some golden nuggets) if it becomes clear you're not a match after all.

The Romance Stage

The romance stage is a chemical high that you experience when falling in love. It's a potent cocktail of dopamine (feel-good hormone), norepinephrine (causing your heart to race), phenylethylamine (neurotransmitter triggering butterflies in your stomach), and serotonin reduction (reducing appetite and triggering infatuation). This drug-induced state can have you feeling giddy, energetic, and euphoric like you're walking on air. All the songs, movies, stories, and poems refer to the romance stage as love; however, it's more like a declaration of what can become long-lasting love if both people continue to choose each other through the other stages of relationship and beyond.

The Romance stage is also where the phrase "love is blind," comes from. Your brain in love tricks you into viewing your partner with rose-colored glasses, potentially excusing bad behavior, ignoring red flags, going along to get along, and ironing out conflict. The thrill of your emotions can have you rushing to the altar while you're still strangers all because of a feeling. You imagine and highlight how similar the two of you are and the apparent synchronicities and coincidences of your coming together. The trap of the romance stage is that you believe it'll last forever along with the delusion that it'll always feel this good.

Mating is instinctual, but monogamy is a social construct—to love someone for a lifetime is a choice.

The trap of the romance stage is that you believe it'll last forever along with the delusion that it'll always feel this good.

Don't make any commitments during this initial stage; it's not the time to pledge your heart or make any life-altering decisions; instead, it's a time to enjoy while you observe. Some romance stages are intense but short, lasting only a few weeks, while others can last up to two years. The romance stage is supposed to be easy and feel good. In a healthy relationship, disagreements are easily overcome and there appear to be no serious issues between you. A truncated romance stage is a signal to move on because you won't be emotionally invested enough to work through your differences. If you can't resolve issues quickly and easily in this stage, there's little hope your relationship will last and/or be fulfilling. The longer the romance stage, the better situated you are for long-lasting love, as this is the fuel in the tank of the relationship that gets you through the next stage.

The cocktail of chemicals in the brain during this stage is nature's way of ensuring survival of the species by generating the desire to mate and procreate. Plus, when two different people come together and procreate, the likelihood of survival of the family unit increases. If you were starting a business, you wouldn't want everyone to have the same skill set; you'd need a variety of people with varying skills for the venture to succeed. A resilient relationship requires contrasting expertise allowing you to defer to one another's strengths to overcome problems. This is why extroverts are attracted to introverts, leader energy balances responder energy, the practical one grounds the free spirit, and the intellectual is drawn to the passionate. It's your differences that create attraction and balance your relationship, an essential element for love to be long-lasting.

The Power Struggle Stage

The chemical high of the romance stage inevitably wears off, and you end up with an emotional hangover. Where your partner was once "perfect for you" and also "just like you," now you're left with an imperfect person who's different than you. What was charming and cute is now annoying and frustrating. The fear that maybe you aren't so perfect together intrudes on the fantasy that you'll never have problems with the "right" person. What once was so exciting is now giving way to a tug-of-war between you as each of you feels the need to fight for your ego desires. The differences that ignited attraction (that you had glossed over in the romance stage) become highlighted. This ego battle requires one of you to be "right," making the other "wrong." You feel like you're fighting for your beliefs, your emotions, and your story of hurt and frustration when you're actually going through a necessary individuation process in your relationship. You temporarily merged into one in the romance stage, and now you're trying to navigate reclaiming your individuality while not losing your relationship. This is the power struggle stage, where each person is fighting for their way of being, or their way of doing things.

Every couple's power struggle is unique to them; some are dramatic and explosive, while others are more like a simmering cold war. Just because you're not outwardly fighting doesn't mean you aren't in a power struggle. The power struggle stage can last anywhere from a couple of months to years, depending on your tolerance for disconnection. This is not a one-off disagreement; this stage is marked by a repetitive cycle. The two of you end up in the same dispute over and over again unless or until you break up or resolve the power struggle and move on to stage three.

The chemical high isn't designed to last forever, and one of the biggest myths of romantic love is that you'll always feel "in love" with your partner. The moment the power struggle emerges you'll wonder if you're with the wrong person. No couple skips the power struggle stage; it's an opportunity to reinvent the relationship. It's a make-or-break stage for your relationship. If you get stuck in the power struggle, your relationship might end before it can mature, or you try to ignore your differences, and eventually you can't do it any longer. This puts you in a lather–rinse–repeat dating cycle of the romance stage—power struggle—breakup, either with the same person or moving on to a new partner. In order to move forward to stage three and break the cycle, you'll have to discover how to navigate your differences.

Statistics from the U.S. Census Bureau report that most divorces occur in the eighth year of marriage; the second highest rate is in years one to two of marriage. The latter makes sense, considering that many couples marry during the romance stage, while they're still wearing rose-colored glasses. Add this statistic from the Gottman Institute to the eight-year mark—the average couple will wait six years before seeking professional help with a relationship-ending problem.

When you realize that no couple skips the power struggle (though for some it's more of a cold war), you're better prepared to approach it with intention instead of annoyance. Our client Stephanie reconnected with Joel (a man she'd known for over twenty-one years), and because of their long acquaintanceship, they quickly moved into an exclusive relationship. They had never both been available for a relationship at the same time before and jumped at the opportunity to finally start dating. It seemed as if they'd already been together for decades due to their comfort and familiarity with each other.

A few months into their relationship, Stephanie reached out because they were fighting a lot and she worried they'd made a mistake. We quickly determined they'd reached the power struggle stage. When we shared with Stephanie our diagnosis, she exclaimed, "I thought we'd skipped the power struggle because we've known each other for so long!" Power struggles are never about how much time you've spent together; they're an indication that your ego desires are taking precedence over the relationship. Disagreements are rarely about the details you're arguing about.

Remember, an intimate relationship can function like a funhouse mirror at a carnival. In a funhouse mirror you see a distorted image of yourself; you might have a long head with a tiny torso and big giant feet, or some other weird likeness staring back at you. What you see is so odd that you don't recognize yourself. This is what can happen in a romantic relationship, particularly during the power struggle stage. That distorted image of yourself, along with all your flaws and frustrations, are projected onto your partner. It's not easy to look at your wounds or your deficiencies; it's so much easier to blame your partner for your upset. By taking responsibility for your emotional reaction, you create space for your partner to meet you at that high vibration of authenticity. This is where true connection and intimacy are built, and trust becomes a healing balm. Your relationship becomes a safe space to share one another's thoughts and feelings and your love grows over time.

The summer Matthew's mother passed away and shortly afterward Orna's soulmate kitty crossed the rainbow bridge, our grief compounded. Under stress and duress, it's normal for people to be less resourceful than usual, and we found ourselves in a power struggle. Having pride in our ability to identify and break patterns, it was humbling that even though we could identify the pattern, we struggled to break it.

One evening during another disagreement we decided to play with it and switch roles: Orna said Matthew's lines and Matthew said Orna's. We wanted to see what we could discover by switching roles, hoping to break out of this cycle. Even though nothing changed from this experiment, we continued leaning on our commitment to never give up on each other and pressed on to find a viable solution that created a win-win (and to be clear, we didn't fight every day, or even every week). Then one day Orna's frustration with Matthew's lack of attention to detail brought the thought, "Why can't he be more conscientious and thoughtful like I am?" The answer landed on her like a bucket of ice-cold water, because in Matthew's family there were few consequences for making a mistake. His parents were lenient and relatively easygoing; however, in Orna's family she was constantly walking on eggshells, never knowing what might set off one of her parents. There were grave consequences for upsetting them. Orna realized that for Matthew to have the same attention to detail as her, he would have had to grow up in a similar environment as her—that was the last thing she would wish on anybody, let alone the man she loved with her whole heart. Orna's upset melted away with this new perspective, and she released the desire for Matthew to be more like her. The realization that she was safe in her home with her husband meant she no longer had to be on high alert holding herself to an unrealistic standard, or constantly reading the room wondering if it was safe to exist. This power struggle came to an end when Orna conceded and told Matthew that he ought to prepare himself to experience some of her mistakes. That night she decided to be more forgetful moving forward and stop cataloging little things that irritated him. She was taking herself off high alert, relaxing, and being more like Matthew. Peace and harmony have been more consistent in our home ever since.

Ultimately, the power struggle stage is an ego tug of war. To grow to the next stage, both people must be willing to have a change in perspective. In a healthy dynamic, each of you makes deposits and withdrawals to the relationship, and by choosing the relationship over your ego desires you're able to drop the rope and end the tug of war. Instead of choosing "me," you start choosing "we." By deferring to one another's strengths, you open the door to create stability in the relationship.

The Stability Stage

Now that you've both chosen to fight for the relationship, you're in it for the long haul. The stability stage is a period of peace in your relationship and begins with giving up trying to change each other. You're accepting and appreciating each other's differences and deferring to one another's strengths. The love between you has deepened and is a more mature love, contrasting the giddy infatuation of the romance stage. It's time to grow your sense of mutual respect and practice healthy boundaries with each other. If you're unable to do this, you're at risk of falling back into the destructive patterns of the power struggle. In this stage you begin to recognize that love is not something you get from your partner, love is something that you share with them. You've released the fantasy that your relationship will always be easy, and you're okay with it because you've created a trusting space to be vulnerable, build intimacy, and heal your core wounds. You've bonded together and may develop a "you and me against the world" mentality, where you've insulated your relationship against outside forces. No longer trying to change each other, a feeling of peace and comfort sets in.

Part of the stability stage is negotiating the details of your life together. A main area of disagreement between couples is about differing standards. You may have exacting standards on how to clean your home, while your partner is much more lax with mess. You could fight with your partner, demanding that they meet your standards for cleanliness and criticize them for their slovenly habits, but that doesn't sound fun or loving. You could grit your teeth and try to live with a messier home, but that's a recipe for anger and resentment. You're never going to get someone to care about something as much as you do. Or you could defer to one another's strengths, trading one task for another. Maybe your partner is good with numbers and can manage your finances, or maybe your partner is a tinkerer who can contribute by fixing items around the house. Instead of fighting with your partner to do it your way, you're looking to create a win-win so that neither of you feels like you're going into sacrifice.

Matthew spent much of his childhood with his mom in the kitchen, and Orna's mom was a professional chef. For both of us, food is love, so much so that many of our disagreements begin in the kitchen. Both of us enjoy cooking and eating healthy food. Early on Orna realized that Matthew didn't just enjoy cooking, he was a bit of a control freak about it. When Orna was cooking, Matthew would come in to help and end up taking over. After we got engaged, Orna made the decision to demote herself to sous chef and told Matthew he could be executive chef for the rest of our lives together, but that she didn't want to be the forever dishwasher. Matthew agreed and said he didn't want to be the trashman. Cleaning up and taking out the garbage is a shared domestic task in our home. It's easy to divide up the tasks of running our business because we both have different strengths and weaknesses. We both get to excel in our zones of genius. Dividing tasks up doesn't just happen because you love each other; you must be willing to have the uncomfortable conversations to create the connection and stability you want from a beloved partnership.

Without continued growth and evolution in your relationship it will stagnate, with boredom increasing and passion decreasing; this is the trap of getting stuck in the stability stage. Your relationship feels secure, but it must keep growing, or it will become stale. Relationship growth requires change and stepping outside your comfort zone. One way you can keep growing together is by consciously creating new shared experiences, traveling, taking dance classes or tantra classes, attending personal development seminars, or anything that keeps you feeling connected and stretches you beyond your ordinary daily life. Dating reality shows often put contestants in extreme situations like hot air balloons, rock climbing, or helicopter rides because the heightened shared experience creates an instant bond. Continue growing together by stepping outside your comfort zone, and your relationship will continue to thrive.

The Commitment Stage

This commitment stage is where you're finally ready to make a lifelong commitment to each other. You've worked through your differences and have skills for navigating conflict and turning it into a deeper connection. You've chosen to fight for the relationship and easily let go of the rope. Now, you're ready to accept your partner, warts and all. It's like you found them at the as-is section at Ikea and you're choosing to take them home and love them, no matter their imperfections. You don't need your partner to change for you to be happy. The commitment stage is best defined by the phrase, "I love you anyway." This means that even though you have your differences, you choose to love each other. You may even come to appreciate those aspects of your partner that annoy you the most. You're choosing love daily and choosing to be loving with each other.

In your relationship, there's a balance of power, love, freedom, and fun that comes with this stage as well as a feeling of belonging—the feeling that home is where your mate is, and your brain chemistry starts producing more oxytocin (the bonding chemical). Your friendship as well as your passion grow more deeply between you. It's important during this stage that you actively work to stay connected with your partner and work through any conflicts that may arise. Despite making this deeper commitment to each other, you can become complacent in your relationship and fall back into past negative patterns. It's at this stage where you're actually ready to make a lifelong commitment to each other. Interestingly enough, this is not your final stage; your relationship has the potential for an even bigger impact in the world.

The Bliss or Co-Creation Stage

At this stage there's so much love between you that you feel compelled to co-create something. Your love is so great that it spills over into your community (or the world) by creating something larger than yourselves. This could mean raising children together, giving back to society through a charity or philanthropy, starting a collaborative project, launching a business together, or helping with a cause close to your hearts. Stage five isn't the end of the line; your relationship doesn't stagnate here. In times of stress, it's common to revert to old patterns and strategies to cope, and this can cause a resurgence of the power struggle. It's also possible for the romance stage to reignite passion and curiosity for one another. In the co-creation stage you've learned that love is not infatuation, love is not power, love is not stability, and love is not commitment. Love is bliss that is meant to be shared with the world. There's a Swedish proverb that sums up this stage perfectly: *Shared joy is double joy. Shared sorrow is half sorrow.* By committing to develop your love and relationship skills you can double your joy and halve your sorrow for a lifetime of love.

> *In the co-creation stage you've learned that love is not infatuation, love is not power, love is not stability, and love is not commitment. Love is bliss that is meant to be shared with the world.*

Rob Thomas, the lead singer of the band Matchbox Twenty, and his wife, Marisol, have been married for over two decades. After the death of their rescue dog, they started the Sidewalk Angels Foundation in 2003 to provide critically needed funding and support to over twenty no-kill animal shelters throughout the United States. The Obama Foundation promotes creating a world that provides girls with an equal chance for education and helps young Black men of color to have clear pathways to opportunity. Michelle and Barack Obama are no strangers to working together to make the world a better place for everyone. George and Amal Clooney cofounded the Clooney Foundation for Justice, which provides free legal support to victims of human rights abuses in over forty countries around the world. These are just a few examples of how the co-creation stage illustrates the expansion of common values beyond just two people who love one another. Your soulmate relationship may not touch tens of thousands of people, but for you and your beloved it will be just right.

The five stages of relationship are not set in stone. Couples move through these stages in order the first time through, and then hopscotch around. You'll keep returning to the power struggle stage until you learn to resolve conflict in a way that builds your partner up instead of tearing them down, establish a reliable emotion connection, repair broken trust and heal old hurts, and accept your partner's flaws and appreciate how they're different than you. Any person can learn the skill set for creating lasting love, and it only takes one person to change the dynamic in a relationship. Mastering these skills becomes part of the toolbox for you to find your way through life together no matter the challenges or curveballs that come your way. Imagine your life with a partner by your side that you can count on no matter what—this is what Creating Love on Purpose produces for you.

LOVE ON PURPOSE EXERCISES

Navigating conflict in your relationship requires you to have tools so that you're more resourceful. These exercises are useful at any stage of relationship, even while dating. Working through your differences is one of the most important skills you can develop for long-lasting love.

Calming Your Nervous System

Attempting to communicate with your partner when you're feeling upset or triggered is a recipe for escalating a conflict. Withdrawing without communication and hoping that the conflict will go away will create unresolved landmines in your relationship that can explode at any moment. Many people think it's their partner's responsibility to calm them down, which is inaccurate. You are the only person responsible for your emotional reactions, and you're the only person capable of calming your own nervous system. The brain controls how you think, learn, move, and feel. When you're upset, your cerebral cortex goes offline, and you're reacting from the amygdala in the base of the brain that controls the fight–flight–freeze response. Becoming skilled at calming your own nervous system is the key to longevity in intimate relationships, because once you're calm, your cerebral cortex will come back online so you can repair and reconnect with your partner.

Some common symptoms that you're not calm include rationalizing or defending your behavior, escalating by increasing volume or being repetitive, shutting down and appearing checked-out, or becoming hypercritical. To soothe yourself, you must first recognize that you're triggered (the earlier the better) so you can calmly repair and reconnect. Being triggered occurs on a dial switch rather than an on–off switch, so you can think of it as a scale of 1–10, and the sooner you identify that you're upset the faster you can work to calm yourself down. Because your breath occurs in the present moment, it is the most effective tool for calming your nervous system. Any type of breathwork, like meditation, is incredibly beneficial because the more you practice being in the present moment, the easier and the faster you'll be able to return to a peaceful state. Bringing conscious intention to your breathing by pacing your inhales and exhales will help you shift from the fight–flight–freeze response of the sympathetic nervous system to the resting response of the parasympathetic nervous system.

First, inform your partner that you need time to calm down and find a space where you can be alone. Lie down comfortably on a couch, bed, or floor. Place your left hand on your navel and your right hand on the center of your chest (your sternum or heart center). Inhale into your navel for a count of two, then exhale for a count of four. As you become more centered and present, increase to breathing in to a count of four and exhaling to a count of eight. (Any combination will work as long as the exhale length is double your inhale.) Continue breathing like this for several minutes until your mind begins to quiet and your body starts to relax. While you're breathing you can repeat an affirmation to occupy your mind and encourage yourself to relax. A couple of our favorites include, "I allow my mind to relax and be at peace. Clarity and harmony are within and around me." Or "Peace, like a river, flows through me, flows through me."

Turning Conflict into a Deeper Connection—The Couch Exercise

Once you've calmed your nervous system, you're now ready to repair, reconnect, and find a way through your differences. We used this process to restore emotional connection after our first big conflict, and it has been one of our most effective tools for navigating our differences to create a deeper connection. Our clients find it a bit funny that we just call it "the couch," because it's best done on a couch. The usefulness of a sofa is that when you start you can sit at each end of the couch and as you work through the issue you can come together in the middle to hold hands, or for a long hug, a kiss, or a make-out session after you're emotionally connected again.

Throughout the couch exercise, each of you will do your best to use "I" language and avoid "You" language. (This is where all the practice you've had with the SHYFT will pay off.) Share your feelings rather than your thoughts, and it's best when you begin with an apology if possible. The agreement is that each person speaks until they say, "I'm done"; that way, there's no interrupting. The person listening comes from a place of compassion and seeks to gain insight and understanding. If you're creating a response in your head, you're no longer listening to your partner (this is a self-policing practice). Continue to take turns speaking and listening while taking responsibility for your triggers and emotional stories.

Eventually, compassion and love enter the space between you, and either of you can make requests to hold hands, to look at one another, to even breathe together. At some point, the details of the disagreement fall from being important and you can ask each other what you need in order to accept an apology, including the opportunity to make amends. The beauty of the couch is that when you each decide that being authentic and compassionate with each other is the goal, you will be emotionally connected again because intimacy does not require agreement.

Scan the QR code for bonus materials and video trainings:

14

The Bridge to Your Beloved

*"We come to love not by finding a perfect person, but by
learning to see an imperfect person perfectly."*

—Sam Keen

No longer blocked by the limiting beliefs, emotional patterns, and
behavioral strategies of Your Love Imprint, you've transformed
false beliefs, healed your core wound from childhood, and have
new strategies for expressing yourself. You've released attachment
to your emotional stories, embraced an empowering inner dialog,
and learned how to love and accept yourself as is. You've mined
the gold of your past relationships, and you have a new connection with your inner child. You've embraced new strategies for dating, explored the energetic dance of the leader and responder,
and have a clear vision of how your true soul partnership will function. The final step is to bridge all these tools together and walk
your unique path to your beloved.

You'll know you've broken the pattern of Your Love Imprint
when a new kind of person piques your interest and curiosity. You
can quickly recognize when a person is a match to Your Love
Imprint and move on without much thought or hesitation. You're
comfortable moving slowly through the dating process, and it
doesn't feel compulsive or out of balance; instead, it has you feeling grounded and attentive. You don't feel the need to rush

because you're afraid of losing a good prospect. You feel an attraction, but your brain remains online, and you can wait until your new dating partner has earned the benefit of the doubt before investing your heart. You no longer feel that you need someone to fill an empty space inside of you, and instead desire to share your life with someone to increase the joy you're already grateful for. You've broken the pattern of Your Love Imprint when you can be rational with your decision making even while feeling the rush and excitement of a new romance.

When Wendy reached out to us, she was 39 years old, divorced from an emotionally unavailable man, and feeling extremely sad, heartbroken, and alone. Filled with worry, she thought time was running out to become a mother and have children of her own. Being a rather quirky, spiritual woman who dabbles in astrology and grows medicinal plants, she always had trouble fitting in. It was seemingly impossible to get a date in her tiny Midwestern community; there just weren't many opportunities to meet guys on her wavelength. As a natural innovator, she lives outside the box as a creative thinker along with some peculiar and unique interests. Personal freedom is very important to Wendy, and it shows up in every area of her life. More than anything, she wanted a partner who shared her sense of adventure. Her unconventionality was part of her childhood and part of her nature. She was raised in Thailand by a Scottish father and an American mother. Her father was emotionally distant from both Wendy and her mother, so her mother sought emotional connection with her. Unfortunately, her mother's love always came with strings attached, creating a sense of longing and a habit of going into sacrifice.

Wendy had difficulty trusting men because she didn't think her father was a good man. He had cheated on his first wife, and in Wendy's mind he wasn't a person with integrity. There was a lot of anger attached to her love imprint, "I don't count or matter in love." Some of that anger originated from her mother's manipulations, but mostly it stemmed from her father's lack of interest in her as well as his lack of character.

Unlike most of our clients, Wendy had no resistance to scheduling and committing to weekly Inner Child Dates; it was right in her wheelhouse. She also took to expressing herself authentically because she inherently didn't have an issue with speaking her mind. The loss of confidence and self-esteem she felt after her divorce was familiar from her childhood, so there was plenty of healing work to release the false belief that no man would ever truly understand her or have the capacity to provide emotional support. She wanted a man who would put in the effort to understand her many complicated layers, someone willing to peel her like an onion. Like many independent, successful women, she was comfortable in her leader energy but longed for a man who would make her feel emotionally safe. She didn't need a man to help pay the bills, but she had no idea what she wanted her beloved to provide for her instead. Through our work together, Wendy leaned into her responder energy through her creativity, and this carried it into her Inner Child Dates, trying on frilly, pretty dresses and having tea parties with dolls.

It was challenging for Wendy to decipher the signals guys were sending her. At one point she developed a crush on her acupuncturist because she mistook his kindness and care for affection, and she kept waiting for him to make a move that never came. It took some time to break the habit of making assumptions and futurizing when she found someone even remotely attractive or appropriate for her. After a couple of awkward experiences, she finally stopped trying to figure out what a guy was thinking and started paying attention to how he was showing up. Wendy's biggest resistance was online dating because she'd had several awful experiences before coming to us. Placing the discovery on herself first, along with our support, finally got her to sign up. She never could have imagined how quickly her life would change by taking the risk of stepping through that very hot door to try dating apps again.

Ray was the second man to reach out to her online. They would have never crossed paths in person because he lived three hours away and never traveled to her part of the state. After several phone calls getting to know each other, he eagerly came to her town for their first date. Wendy had embraced the idea that she should let her freak flag fly so her beloved could find her, so she told him how much she loved adventure. To her delight, he surprised her by taking her bungee jumping on her birthday early in the dating process. Several weeks later they spent the day at one of her favorite places on Earth, a lake that's very special to Wendy. They had a wonderful time on the water, hiked the woods around the lake, and had a picnic lunch in a lush meadow. Later Wendy remembered having written one of her ideal scenes at the lake and was astonished that her real-life experience with Ray matched the vision she had created in the exercise. They married right there on the lake about a year later with a small group of friends, and with Wendy's spiritual teacher as the officiant. Wendy tells Ray all the time that without Creating Love on Purpose they would never have been together. After their daughter was born, Wendy asked Ray if he would be interested in being partners in her business. That was more than a decade ago, and they plan to continue their unconventional lifestyle by living out of an RV and homeschooling their child, committing to a nomadic lifestyle for the next several years.

You get to craft your true soul partnership. There's no one-size-fits-all when it comes to relationships and how they function. Each of our clients has a unique journey to their beloved, and their soulmate relationship reflects who they are and their preferred lifestyle. Set your intention for love; create a clear vision of what it looks like along with how it functions to discover the evidence you'll need to know you've found your soulmate. Continue taking actions through warm and hot doors to stretch out of your comfort zone. Commit to viewing your emotions as information rather than something that inspires action. Master uncomfortable conversations by taking the risk to speak your feelings and make requests. It's never too early to share your truth; better to find out as soon as possible if you two can find your way through the rough spots together.

You get to craft your true soul partnership. There's no one-size-fits-all when it comes to relationships and how they function.

Your mantra as you navigate dating, through exclusivity, to a commitment is always, "This, or better." When you meet someone promising, remember you don't yet know if this person is your beloved. Instead of getting emotionally attached, remind yourself if it's not this person, then it will be someone even better. Every "No" is leading you closer to your "Yes." And every relationship that doesn't work out is full of gold for you to move forward and become a better person, more capable and resilient to create the lasting love you desire. Each promising prospect is not a unicorn; you don't have to hang on tight just because this is the best person you've found so far. Ultimately, you can't say or do the wrong thing with the right person. With your soulmate, you'll find your way through the

Ultimately, you can't say or do the wrong thing with the right person.

misunderstandings and miscommunications that occur. If you can't find your way back to each other, then there's someone better suited for you.

Asking you to date with nonattachment doesn't mean that you're indifferent through the process. If you're interested and enjoying their company, let them know—flirt! Be your authentic self, just don't rush into exclusivity or physical intimacy. If your responsive energy is dominant, lean back and relax, and be receptive. If your leading energy is dominant, move the relationship forward by initiating dates and communication in between. Be up front and honest about continuing to date other people. If you want to shift from your negative patterns, use the SHYFT. Sharing your feelings and making requests allows you to evaluate a person's capacity to meet your needs.

Olivia had no trouble getting dates. She spent a weekend overswiping and had dates lined up for more than two weeks. One guy in the rotation was giving her pause; Olivia would find him very attractive on one date, and not so attractive on another. The largest erogenous zone is the space between your ears—your brain. We realized that Olivia spent a lot of brainpower constantly trying to find out what was going on in this guy's head. Her sharp mind was not an ally in the search for long-lasting love, as she would end up in analysis paralysis every time the chemistry was piqued. Once she stopped wondering what was going on with him and focused on herself and her feelings, it became clear that he was part of her old pattern of choosing flaky guys. Her overthinking was a strategy of convincing herself that her intuition about him was wrong and was part of a pattern of not trusting herself. Oliva's realization allowed her to quickly deselect him and move on in her dating life. It also became a stepping-stone to learning to trust her gut.

The beauty and ease of going on this journey to create love on purpose is that you don't have to analyze your dates for a potential match. You'll never be able to know accurately and consistently what's going on in someone else's head. Couples who have been happily married for decades still surprise one another. Every now and then in our house we have an "opposite day" where Orna's response is more like Matthew's and vice-versa. If you want to discover whether a person is your long-term match, share what's going on with you and take note of how they respond. All you need to do to shift your love life for good is to embrace the SHYFT communication blueprint. It sounds simple, but it may not be easy, and that's why it's essential you practice right from the moment you first interact with a prospect. Get out of your head (we know it's served you well in other areas of your life) and get into your body and into your feeling state. Embrace the SHYFT to discover your soulmate.

Once you find your soulmate, the lights won't fade to black as you imagine your happily ever after; you still have the rest of your lives together. You and your beloved will be two different people walking the same path, sharing a life together that's better than you can imagine right now—not because they complete you, but because they'll function as your ally in life, you'll heal each other's wounds, and you'll feel inspired to be your best self. The high of the romance stage will seem somewhat shallow compared to the deep love you have for each other after years and decades together. Will your beloved also drive you bonkers sometimes? Yes, of course, you'll be sharing your life with someone, and disagreements and conflict will always be part of your dance together. What you get in return is like exchanging whatever cash you currently have in your wallet for a treasure chest of gold. When you stick it out with someone long term, you'll reap immeasurable rewards.

We have no way of knowing exactly what being with your beloved will feel like for you, but we can tell you that it won't feel like Your Love Imprint match. It won't feel all-consuming, or obsessive, or filled with anxiety; instead, it'll feel comfortable, easy, and relaxed. Orna vehemently dislikes the saying, "When you know, you know," about finding the right person. At twenty-seven years old, she thought she knew, but it was the worst decision she had ever made, and it almost cost her life. As we mentioned at the beginning of our journey together, Orna's been interviewed hundreds of times, and people often ask her, "How did you know it was Matthew? How did you know he was the one?" The only way to put it into words is to describe how it felt for her. She didn't have all the angst she usually had at the beginning of a relationship. She didn't second guess herself or overthink things; instead, it was super easy and comfortable. For the first time, falling in love felt grounded, like she had the roots of a giant oak tree that went deep into Mother Earth, and at the same time she felt like she had wings, and she could take flight at any time. Having roots and wings let her know that Matthew was the one for her. It wasn't like anything else she had ever experienced before. Will you have roots and wings when you come together with your soulmate? You may not describe it exactly same way, and we can't wait for you to find out and share it with us!

Once you've reached the commitment stage with your soul-mate, they've earned the benefit of the doubt. Even when they've upset you or disappointed you, they didn't intend to hurt you. Every person you love deserves to have a bad day, and you can let things slide when they do. Accepting your imperfections is prac-tice for living with an imperfect person as your soulmate. A soul-mate isn't fated or destined; they're someone who accepts you as you are, who gets you, and who stands by you. Plus, there's wonderful emotional and physical intimacy that's present. You and your soulmate never grow apart because you choose love every day, and your love grows deeper over time.

> *You and your soulmate never grow apart because you choose love every day, and your love grows deeper over time.*

The year we got married we were on a tight budget with a wedding to pay for, so we decided not to exchange Valentine's Day gifts. After a lovely day together bike riding and making pizza from scratch, we sat down after dinner and Orna gave Matthew a card. Having read the sweet note inside, he sat there uncomfortably and stated he didn't have anything for her. He had taken the agreement literally, as in we're not exchanging anything, not even cards. Like in a movie scene, Orna's eyes filled up with tears and then slowly started spilling over like a light rain on her cheeks. Soon she couldn't contain her disappointment, got up and flung herself on the bed in a big ugly cry. After a bit of sobbing, there was a gentle knock on the door and Matthew asked if he could come in. He held her tightly and apologized profusely, stroking her hair, and brushing back her tears. Finally, she said, "I just never thought you would break my heart." Matthew promised to make it up to her, and Orna accepted that they'd had a misunderstanding. The next morning he'd left a note on her car apologizing once again for their miscommunication and vowed to make amends.

That evening Matthew gave Orna a card, not a Valentine's Day card, but one that was meaningful to her with a handwritten note inside, instituting "Orna Banarie Appreciation Month." For the next thirty-one days she received a card from Matthew *every single day*. Every card expressed an aspect of Orna's character that he appreciated. Even when she was in a bad mood, regardless of how the day had gone between them (with or without bumps), even when they'd stayed out late with friends, the cards didn't stop coming. Even when Orna thought there just couldn't be anything more to say or appreciate about her, they kept coming. She'd been upset about not receiving *one card on one day*, and now she was receiving cards daily for a full month on the calendar—thirty-one days! After all the personal growth workshops she'd invested in and having exercised her receiving muscles, Orna couldn't believe she'd hit a glass ceiling. She started to feel undeserving of the love bestowed upon her by her fiancée. Taking deep breaths and walking through a very hot door, Orna decided to just let Matthew give all his love to her. She didn't protest or renegotiate, or try to reciprocate; she just allowed him to do what he promised—to make it up to her. When we say your heart breaks open to hold more love, we know this is true from our own experience. These thirty-one days broke Orna's heart wide open, and it's never shrunk back since.

Where can you break through the glass ceiling in your love life? How can you utilize all the tools and practices and discovery about yourself to let love in? Love is messy, and it requires risk. Ironically, parents don't hold it against their children when they literally defecate and vomit on them, and they don't withdraw their love. You can extend forgiveness to your beloved when they make a mistake, when they're not wired like you are, and when they disappoint you. It's in the repair that love grows deeper, and that's why it's called "growing pains." Having the uncomfortable conversations will always bring you closer together when you're with the right person. This is exactly what makes them your soulmate—because they want to work it out *with you*. The person who is willing to apologize and make amends is the person worth keeping. Your love resiliency doesn't grow through the good times—they are their own reward. Instead, your love grows through the challenges you face. Don't see them as obstacles to having love; they are the pathway to having the greatest love of your life.

Always in forgiveness is a vow worth taking with your beloved. "Wabi sabi" is the Japanese worldview of finding beauty in imperfection and impermanence. Our client Orly reached out to us, incredulous that she'd asked her boyfriend Jack to put his shoes away repeatedly, and she was adamant that she'd used the SHYFT. After moving in together they agreed to have their home a shoeless household. The good news was, he regularly took his shoes off and honored their lifestyle choice. We reminded her that the SHYFT is not a magical template that makes people behave the way you want them to. After many requests and equally as many agreements, she found his shoes piled up at the front door, and she felt angry and resentful that she had to put them away. Now she was worried after putting in all the time with him that Jack maybe wasn't the right guy for her after all. We talked her off the ledge by asking several questions about how he treats her, like when they've had disagreements, or when she'd had a bad day at work. We asked about their overall dynamic with each other.

The good news was they appeared to be in alignment with all four tenets for relationship longevity: attraction, compatible lifestyles, shared values, and communication. The bad news was she had no control over the differences in the execution of those four tenets. He clearly liked living in a shoeless household; their differences included that it didn't bother him to have his shoes piled up by the door; that's something that only bothered her. She didn't *have to* put them away; she was choosing to do that. His willingness and desire to please her by saying he would regularly take them back to the closet illustrated how much he cares for her, but unfortunately, you can't change what's important to someone. Plus, this isn't some life-threatening situation.

To Jack, the shoes piled up at the door were convenient and somewhat efficient. Because it bothered her, it was up to her to do something about it. We decided to guide Orly to have a change of perspective. Was it worth giving up on Jack and all that they'd been through together because he left his shoes by the door? She was clear this was not a deal-breaker. Her celebrity crush was Kevin Bacon, and she knew if she was shacked up with Mr. Bacon, he could leave his shoes by the door every day of the week—so she was going to have to find another way. We asked her to come up with some things that Jack did for her that no man had ever done before. She answered our questions about their love life and whether it was satisfying and yummy. We went over her values and asked if they were still a majority match. He checked all the boxes—she said she got more than she had ever imagined.

We asked Orly to picture Jack out of her life and how it would feel to move on. Then we asked, "Can you decide that you *get to* put Jack's shoes away?" Bottom line, she lived with this guy named Jack whom she declared to love, and he loved her back. Because they shared a household, there's proof that he's there every night with his shoes piled up at the door. Orly decided that it's well worth it to put Jack's shoes back in the closet when she tidied up. She also made a vision board to imagine a future home for them with a foyer (instead of the tiny one-bedroom apartment they were sharing), and she even clipped out a photo of an entry-way hall tree with a bench to sit on, hooks to hang coats, cubbies to store shoes, umbrellas, hats, and so forth. This is what we call "wabi sabi love" from Arielle Ford's book of the same name. It's not perfect, but you love it anyway—just like we said earlier that if you found it as-is at Ikea you'd take it home and be thrilled with the deal you got—plus it's already assembled. Wabi sabi those annoyances about your partner after they've proved to be worthy and have earned the benefit of the doubt. Now is the time to pull out your rose-colored glasses that you stashed while you were dating and see your loving partner in the best light.

You get to create your soulmate relationship, no matter your past or present circumstances. It doesn't matter where you live, how old you are, how much money you have, how attractive you are (and whatever other excuses you can think of)—love is waiting for you. It's always been there. We know that you are worth loving; just by existing you deserve love. There's no higher power keeping love from you. Now you have the tools and new strategies to manifest it. No matter the setbacks on your journey to long-lasting love, remember that you are worth loving!

LOVE ON PURPOSE EXERCISE—ACTING AS IF

One of the most powerful exercises we ask our clients to do is to "act as if"—acting as if you already have what you desire. In the way you think, dress, walk, plan your day, you're moving through the world as if you're already with your beloved (or that it's inevitable). Acting as if allows you to build self-confidence, trains your subconscious, and creates a self-fulfilling prophecy. Giving your subconscious mind specific instructions allows your subconscious to highlight the evidence of your goal. You can think of it as lighting the pathway to your beloved by simply moving through the world as if it's already true.

Ask yourself these questions, and journal your responses:

1. What if I knew my soulmate was already here, waiting for me?
2. What if it was just a matter of time before we met in person and my job was to be present in the world in order to be seen?
3. How would I act differently?
4. How would I carry myself in the world?

5. How would I respond to a date not working out or to someone rejecting me?

Your soulmate is waiting for you to become the person you need to be to receive the love you desire and deserve. Start acting "as if" this were true, and you'll find yourself more emotionally resilient and less prone to burn-out and frustration. You'll take every setback as an opportunity to grow and do better. You'll be grateful for the experiences you'll have on the way to long-lasting love. You'll be ready when your soulmate finally arrives.

Scan the QR code for bonus materials and video trainings:

ACKNOWLEDGMENTS

To all our clients, thank you for your courage to seek a new way to do love. Without you we wouldn't have a book to share with the world. Thank you for trusting us and allowing us to be your guides. Watching you blossom has been our honor and our pleasure beyond words.

Melanie Gorman, thank you for being our champion, cheerleader, guide, teacher, and friend. We shudder to think where we'd be without your support. You have been the scaffolding that has allowed us to grow with a solid foundation. Thank you for generously sharing your talents with us.

Rori Raye, thank you for giving us a jumpstart simply because you had faith in us. We are forever grateful to you for launching us onto the world stage and for always sharing your wisdom with us.

Tons of gratitude for our literary dream team: Linda, Leslie, and Laura.

Linda Sivertsen, book mama extraordinaire, thank you for sticking with us, for giving us the good news along with the bad, for believing in us and our desire to spread our message of love.

Our agent, Leslie Meredith at Dystel, Goderich, and Bourret, thank you for challenging us in the best ways possible and for believing in us and our message. Your tenacity is as legendary as you are.

Our editor, Laura Apperson, and the team at Alcove Press, Crooked Lane Books, and Penguin Random House. Thank you for believing in our book and making our author dreams come true.

Thank you to everyone who played a part in some version of this book and its gestation including Christine Whitmarsh, Robin Colucci, Geoffrey Berwind, Steve and Laura Harrison, Patty Aubrey, and Jack Canfield.

To all the wonderful writers at the Carmel Writing Retreat, you lifted us up, made our ideas better, and supported the vision of becoming published authors.

Heartfelt gratitude to Berny Dohrmann, founder of CEO Space, for giving us a safe space to develop our business acumen, and our entire entrepreneurial family: September Dohrmann, Maria Speth, Michelle Anton, Michal Mael, Sherita Herring, Adryenn Ashley, Chris Salter, Chimene Holmes, Cheryl Brenner, Jill Lublin, David Fagan, Eve Hogan, Lauren Solomon, and the countless others who were there at the beginning and supported our vision.

Jeneth Blackert, thank you for your friendship and endless support in helping us reach the masses with our mission. You handed us the toolbox to build our platform; we are forever grateful.

Andrea Miller and the entire team at YourTango.com. We're so proud of being OG YT Experts and so very grateful for all the collaborative wins we've had together. Thank you so very much for all the opportunities you've given us.

Moon Zappa, thank you for seeing us as writers and continually nudging us to become published authors. We are so very grateful for your friendship and oodles of your delicious teas to keep us fueled through many long days and nights.

Jonathon Shaevitz, thank you for your friendship and all the guidance and support through many years.

Dr. Susan Campbell, thank you for your guidance, mentorship, and wisdom. We are grateful for all the lessons, especially to always remember the love between us and our commitment to our sacred partnership.

Carol Allen, we are incredibly appreciative of your friendship, for your generous nature, and for all the many connections and introductions you've made on our behalf across numerous years, and for including us in the Homie Hookup.

The one and only Homie Hookup, thank you for collaborating with us.

Damona Hoffman, thank you for being willing to share your journey with us every step of the way so we could learn and grow alongside you. We cherish our friendship and value your support.

Thank you to all the experts who participated in our Love On Purpose Revolution® and joined our mission to bust the myth that love doesn't happen by accident, especially our repeat guests: John Gray, Rhonda Britten, Carol Allen, Evan Marc Katz, Marci Shimoff, Damona Hoffman, Marni Battista, Mat Boggs, Ali Victor Binazir, Debi Berndt and Dr. Robert Maldonado, Cherry Norris, Crystal Hughes, Larry Michel, Marcy Neumann, Jonathon Aslay, Dr. Sheri Meyers, Allana Pratt, Arielle Ford, and Dr. Margaret Paul.

Thanks to everyone at WRS who witnessed the beginning of our relationship and supported us in coming together as a couple.

All of our exes who helped spur each of us on our journey to create lasting love: We're grateful for the motivation you gave us to grow into the people we are today.

All of our family, friends and colleagues who believed in us and shared their support along the way: John and Gloria Walters,

Rhonda Britten, David Lapan, Michelle Weimer, Lorrie Kazan, Nita Vallens, Travis Houston, Myke Smith, Sujon Datta, Elea Oberon, Deborah Madick, Amy Wenslow and Jeff Fretz, Dan and Carol Eagle, Karen Coler-Castaneda, Sara Chameides, Melissa Kolaks Broaddus, Samantha Bennett, Chellie Campbell, Natalie Ledwell, Deborah Kagan, Sally Landau, Helene Lerner, Ian Mankowski, Harrison Morton, Barbara Miller Wood, Charlie and Peggy Werner, Korenna Reynard, Christine Arylo and Noah Martin, Scott and Kathy Nolind, Melissa Yamaguchi, Elisa Van Arnam, Heather Edmondson, Samantha Barracca, David Hurwitz, and John and Kathleen Allee.

Our guru, Paramahansa Yogananda and our spiritual family at the Self-Realization Fellowship. Your teachings have guided us through every step of this journey. OM Shanti OM.

BIBLIOGRAPHY

Andreas, Connie Rae, and Steve Andreas. *Heart of the Mind: Engaging Your Inner Power to Change with NLP*. Moab, UT: Real People Press, 1989.

Andreas, Steve, and Charles Faulkner. *NLP: The New Technology of Achievement*. New York: Quill, 1996.

Baker, Laura A. "The Biology of Relationships: What Behavioral Genetics Tells Us About Interactions Among Family Members." National Library of Medicine, December 21, 2015. https://www.ncbi.nlm.nih.gov/pmc/articles/PMC4685725/

Bieber, Christie J. D. "Leading Causes of Divorce: 43% Report Lack of Family Support." *Forbes*, August 15, 2023. https://www.forbes.com/advisor/legal/divorce/common-causes-divorce/

Bieber, Christie J. D. "Divorce Statistics in 2024." *Forbes*, January 8, 2024. https://www.forbes.com/advisor/legal/divorce/divorce-statistics

Booth, Jessica. "Dating Statistics and Facts in 2024." *Forbes*, February 19, 2024. https://www.forbes.com/health/dating/dating-statistics/

Breathnach, Sarah Ban. *Simple Abundance: 365 Days to a Balanced and Joyful Life*. New York: Grand Central Publishing, 1995.

Cameron, Julie. *The Artist's Way: A Spiritual Path to Higher Creativity*. Los Angeles: Tarcher/Putnam, 1992.

Campbell, Joseph. *The Hero With a Thousand Faces*. Princeton: Princeton University Press, 1949.

Campbell, Susan D., and John Grey. *Five-Minute Relationship Repair: Quickly Heal Upsets, Deepen Intimacy, and Use Differences to Strengthen Love*. Tiburon, CA: HJ Kramer, 2015.

Campbell, Susan D. *From Triggered to Tranquil: How Self-Compassion and Mindful Presence Can Transform Relationship Conflicts and Heal Childhood Wounds.* Novato, CA: New World Library, 2021.

Campbell, Susan D., and John Grey. *The Couple's Journey: Intimacy as a Path to Wholeness.* Oakland, CA: Impact Publishers, 1980.

Canfield, Jack. *The Success Principles: How to Get from Where You Are to Where You Want to Be.* New York: Harper Collins, 1995.

Carlson, Jon, Richard E. Watts, and Michael Maniacci. *Adlerian Therapy: Theory and Practice.* Washington: American Psychological Association, 2005.

De Phillips, Frank Anthony, William M. Berliner, and James J. Cribbin. *Management of Training Programs.* Homewood, IL: Richard D. Irwin, 1960.

Deida, David. *The Way of the Superior Man: A Spiritual Guide to Mastering the Challenges of Women, Work, and Sexual Desire.* Louisville, CO: Sounds True, 1997.

Franken, Al. *I'm Good Enough, I'm Smart Enough, and Doggone It, People Like Me!: Daily Affirmations by Stuart Smalley.* New York: Dell, 1992.

Ford, Arielle. *Wabi Sabi Love: The Ancient Art of Finding Perfect Love in Imperfect Relationships.* New York: Harper One, 1994.

Goleman, Daniel. *Emotional Intelligence: Why It Can Matter More Than IQ.* New York: Bantam, 1995.

Gottman, John M. *What Predicts Divorce? The Relationship Between Marital Processes and Marital Outcomes.* Hillsdale, NJ: Lawrence Erlbaum Associates, 1994.

Hawkins, David R. *Power vs. Force: The Hidden Determinants of Human Behavior.* Carlsbad, CA: Hay House, 2002.

Hay, Louise L. *You Can Heal Your Life.* Carlsbad, CA: Hay House, 1999.

Heller, Steven, and Terry Steele. *Monsters and Magical Sticks: There's No Such Thing as Hypnosis.* Tempe, AZ: New Falcon Publications, 1987.

Hendrix, Harville, and Helen LaKelly Hunt. *Getting the Love You Want: A Guide for Couples.* New York: St. Martin's Publishing Group, 1988.

Hendrix, Harville, and Helen LaKelly Hunt. *Keeping the Love You Find: A Personal Guide.* New York: Atria Books, 1993.

Indelicato, Maria. "In What Year of Marriage Is Divorce Most Common?" April 29, 2023. https://www.marriage.com/advice/divorce/what-year-of-marriage-is-divorce-most-common/

Jung, Carl. *The Stages of Life: The Structure and Dynamics of the Psyche.* (Collected Works, Vol. 8.) Princeton: Princeton University Press, 1969.

Kahneman, Daniel. *Thinking Fast and Slow.* New York: Farrar, Straus and Giroux, 2011.

Kappas, John G. *Success Is Not an Accident: The Mental Bank Concept*. Tarzana, CA: Panaroma, 1987.

Kappas, John G. *Professional Hypnotism Manual: A Practical Approach to Modern Times*. Tarzana, CA: Panaroma Publishing Co., 1987.

Laslocky, Meghan. *The Little Book of Heartbreak: Love Gone Wrong Through the Ages*. New York: Plume, 2012.

Levine, Amir, and Rachel Heller. *Attached: The New Science of Adult Attachment and How It Can Help You Find—and Keep—Love*. New York: TarcherPerigree, 2010.

Levine, Peter A., Ann Frederick. *Waking the Tiger: Healing Trauma*. Berkely: North Atlantic Books, 1997.

McBride, Karyl. *Will I Ever Be Good Enough: Healing the Daughters of Narcissistic Mothers*. New York: Free Press, 2008.

Millman, Dan. *Way of the Peaceful Warrior: A Book That Changes Lives*. Tiburon, CA: HJ Kramer, 1984.

Millman, Dan. *The Life You Were Born to Live*. Tiburon, CA: HJ Kramer, 1993.

Peck, M. Scott. *The Road Less Traveled: A New Psychology of Love, Traditional Values and Spiritual Growth*. New York: Simon & Schuster, 1978.

Muller, Wayne. *The Spiritual Gifts of a Painful Childhood*. Louisville, CO: Sounds True, 1997.

Pert, Candace. *Molecules of Emotion: Why You Feel the Way You Feel*. New York: Scribner, 1997.

Pinker, Steven. *How the Mind Works*. New York: W. W. Norton & Company, 1997.

Poe, Edgar Allen. *The System of Doctor Tarr and Professor Fether*. Graham's Magazine, 1845.

Rosenberg, Marshall. *Nonviolent Communication: A Language of Life: Life-Changing Tools for Healthy Relationships*. Encinitas: PuddleDancer Press, 1999.

Ruiz, Don Miguel. *The Four Agreements: A Practical Guide to Personal Freedom (A Toltec Wisdom Book)*. San Rafael, CA: Amber-Allen Publishing, 1997.

Streep, Peg. *Mean Mothers: Overcoming the Legacy of Hurt*. New York: William Morrow, 2009.

Vaish, Amrisha, Tobias Grossman, and Amanda Woodward. "Not All Emotions Are Created Equal: The Negativity Bias in Social-Emotional Development." National Library of Medicine, May 2008. https://pubmed.ncbi.nlm.nih.gov/18444702

Welwood, John. *Toward a Psychology of Awakening: Buddhism, Psychotherapy, and the Path of Personal and Spiritual Transformation*. Boulder, CO: Shambala Publications, 2000.

Wolinsky, Stephen, and Margaret O. Ryan. *Trances People Live: Healing Approaches in Quantum Psychology*. Falls Village, CT: The Bramble Company, 1991.

Young, Larry, and Alexander Brian. *The Chemistry Between Us: Love, Sex, and the Science of Attraction*. New York: Penguin, 2104.

INDEX